When Our Plane . Hit the

MOUNTAIN

Suzanne Barnes was born in Birmingham in 1950. She studied biological sciences at the University of East Anglia. She lives in Dublin.

When Our Plane Hit the
MOUNTAIN

A True Story

Suzanne Barnes

NEW ISLAND

For Paddy

When Our Plane Hit the Mountain
First published 2005
by New Island
16 Priory Office Park
Stillorgan
Co. Dublin, A94 RH10
Ireland
www.newisland.ie

Reprinted 2019

ISBN 978 1 904301 73 8

British Library Cataloguing in Publication Data. A CIP catalogue record for this book is available from the British Library.

Typeset by New Island
Front cover photograph: courtesy of Geneviève Carrière
Back cover photograph: courtesy of Ministère des affairs étrangères - Nantes
Cover design by New Island
Printed in Ireland by Sprint Print

The publishers have made every reasonable effort to contact the copyright holders of the photographs contained herein. If any involuntary infringement of copyright has occurred, sincere apologies are offered and the owners of such copyright are requested to contact the publishers.

10 9 8 7 6 5 4 3 2

Contents

List of Passengers and Crew   vi

Preface   vii

Prologue   I

Part I   5

Part II   211

Part III   219

Maps   243

Appendixes

   1 Technical Details of Ju-52/3M, *Tante Ju*   246

   2 Extract from and Transcript of Wireless
      Operator's Log   247

   3 Some Important Dates in the History of
      Guiding in Ireland and France   251

   4 Useful Addresses   253

Bibliography   256

Passengers and Crew

GUIDES DE FRANCE

Chantal de Vitry	twenty-one years	Paris
Janine Alexandre	sixteen years	Saint Lô
Geneviève Bétrancourt	seventeen years	Sainte Adresse
Andrée Bonnet	twenty years	Issoire
Françoise Béchet	eighteen years	Avranches
Jacqueline Conort	sixteen years	Le Havre
Antoinette Emo	seventeen years	Le Havre
Catherine de Geuser	fourteen years	Le Havre
Agnès Laporte	seventeen years	Le Havre
Odile Lecoquière	seventeen years	Le Havre
Anne Lemonnier	fifteen years	Yvetot
Eliane Lemonnier	seventeen years	Cherbourg
Antoinette Nattier	sixteen years	Valognes
Odile Stahlberger	fourteen years	Yvetot
Monique Ygouf	fifteen years	Sainte Mère Eglise

ECLAIREUSES

Lilette Levy-Bruhl	twenty-two years	Paris
Micheline Bourdeauducq	eighteen years	Vincennes
Ginette Martin	seventeen years	Nantes
Magali Noyer	seventeen years	Paris
Sylvia Ostrowetsky	thirteen years	Gentilly
Nicole Jacques-Léon	fourteen years	Grenoble

CREW

Christian Habez	twenty-nine years	pilot
Michel Tourret	twenty-seven years	co-pilot
Daniel Duran	twenty-eight years	wireless operator
Georges Biagioni	thirty-three years	navigator
Antoinette de Brimont	twenty-nine years	air hostess

Preface

When a calamity occurs, whether natural or man-made, it is the individual stories – small but epic stories of courage and survival – that persist. This book is about a remarkable incident that happened in 1946 and it is based on the stories of those involved or those who knew them.

The book concerns a group of ordinary teenagers who grew up in war-torn France. It recounts what happened to them when they found themselves caught up in a catastrophic event while travelling by plane from Paris to Dublin.

It was not my purpose to write the biographies of the protagonists, rather to focus on a single day that, for better or worse, had a far-reaching effect on their lives.

My interest in the story arose after a short piece I had written – loosely based on the event – was broadcast on RTÉ radio in February 2003. The following week, I received several phone calls and letters from a cross-section of listeners.

Members of The Irish Girl Guides contacted me and a former Guide, Muriel Webster, invited me to her home to meet other Guides from this period. They showed me original press cuttings, brown and flaky with age, and photographs of the stricken aircraft. The articles made compelling reading. Interest in the story more than fifty years later had also resulted in a radio interview, a short documentary film on RTÉ television and articles in the national press.

I received letters from individuals who had taken part in a dramatic rescue operation in the hills and was chastened to discover that, although the event did not seem to be widely known about outside the area, amongst the local community it had become part of folk culture.

In March 2003, armed with a Dictaphone and dictionary, I embarked on a journey of discovery in Ireland, France and England. The majority of people I spoke to were happy to tell me their version of events. Those I was unable to meet wrote to me describing their experiences, adding personal anecdotes for extra colour. There were, of course, many people with whom I did not speak, either because they had passed away or because I could not find them. Such untapped possibilities, in a book of this nature, will inevitably be unquantifiable.

Stepping quite outside my own field of knowledge, I sought the skills and advice of a range of experts to explain the technical aspects of the flight; and walking on and off trails, I returned many times to the same area in County Wicklow as the yellow gorse faded and the dark greens of summer gave way to the browns of winter and myriad colours in between.

Recollections occur in flashes. It is difficult to keep any chronological order when recording fragments of them and, until I started to weave the ragged threads of individual stories with the innumerable tiny facts I had accumulated along the way, I had not appreciated what a hotchpotch the memory could be. Not surprisingly, the newspaper reports were often as unreliable as people's memories. While I wanted to be as faithful as possible to each person's tale, for the sake of narrative continuity – and occasionally for dramatic effect – I sometimes had to bend an account to fit with certain known facts.

This book would never have seen the light of day without the help and cooperation of all the people that I spoke to.

First and foremost, I would like to thank my dear friend Wendy Dowling. Much of the correspondence and many of the conversations were conducted in French and without her fluent language skills the project would have foundered from the start. She travelled with me to Paris, Le Havre, Nantes and Lille and was unstinting in the time she devoted to translating letters and other archive material.

From The Irish Girl Guides, my thanks to Margaret McKenna, Linda Peters and Jillian van Turnhout. Margaret Dunne allowed me access to archive material. Former Guide Dorothy Mills (*née* Jolley) wrote to me about the accident and I am grateful to her for her graphic description of what happened.

Muriel Webster (*née* Berry), in whose sitting-room the idea of writing a book took hold, introduced me to other members of the Guiding community from 1946 and was instrumental in pointing me towards many people connected with the episode.

I would like to thank Doreen Bradbury, Anne Bowen (*née* Jones), Mona Heary, Mary Henry, Betty Halpin (*née* Moylan) and Rosaline Byrne for their interesting contributions and Phil O'Keefe (*née* Crowley) for her own recollections of the event.

Over an enjoyable lunch in the house that she had shared with her aunt in 1946, Margaret Hamilton-Reid – an energetic ninety-year-old – regaled me with manifold stories from her youth, painting a vivid picture of Ireland in the early part of the twentieth century. For additional information on Guiding in Ireland, I am indebted to Olive McKinley (*née* Sutton), who also gave me a delightful account of her experiences as a teenager in Dublin in the forties.

Much of my research involved linking the past with the present and Eileen Whooley helped me to bridge this gap.

For patiently explaining the intricacies of flight navigation I am beholden to Sean Swords, who went to enormous trouble to render complex technical data into plain English for me. His enthusiasm for the project led him, not only to spend much time explaining 'magnetic declination', 'Gee chains' and other terminology, but also to research the pre-Christian origins of local place names, information that I was able to put to good use in the text. He is also responsible for unravelling the radio-operator's log included in the appendix.

For further technical advice, I am very grateful to Graham Liddy of the Air Accident Investigation Unit in Dublin for his interest and for the archive material he put at my disposal. I am much obliged to Dennis Burke for sending me details on the aircraft involved.

The articles by Bill Nelson and Dermot James were valuable sources of information and both generously elaborated on their original texts for me.

Philip Harvey kindly put me in touch with Mabel Coogan and her mother (also Mabel) who provided me with a wealth of contacts in Enniskerry.

I would like to thank Bill Deely, whose own story is worthy of a book in itself. It was a pleasure to meet Mark, Margaret and Alan Hogan, children of the late Brian Hogan of the former Mount Maulin Hotel, and Michael, son of Conor Hogan. The welcome I received from Mark, Margaret and Alan was, I am sure, as warm as that given to guests in 1946, and I thank them for allowing me to use extracts from their father's written account.

I would like to acknowledge Deirdre Burns of Wicklow County Council and Colm Galligan of the Roundwood Historical Society. Grainne Langrishe and Anne Fitzpatrick provided vital information on the Deerpark. Sean Woodcock and Madge Molloy (*née* Carroll) added further interesting details.

Pat O'Brien and Patrick 'Pa' Brennan were kind enough to relate their parts in the episode. Their reminiscences of growing up in forties Ireland were marvellously evocative. From Pat O'Brien I gained an insight into the hardships of cutting turf on the bog during the Emergency; from Pa Brennan I came to appreciate the landscape of County Wicklow and was taught more about poaching than I would ever care to repeat. I would also like to mention Pearce Kenny, whose own involvement in the episode only came to my attention just before the publication of this book.

I am indebted to Paul Rowan for his account of the event. He rightly suggested he should have been given 'a button hole decoration by the French authorities' for his efforts.

Although I wrote to Arthur Tomkins explaining that I was hoping to include his observations in my book, because of his advanced age I hardly expected a reply. I received a typed letter by return of post. 'What a pleasant surprise today,' he wrote, 'when I received your letter which recalled a foggy day in 1946 but I still have a good memory of things that happened in my experience a long time ago ... so here goes.' The letter continued for two pages. 'If I live until next Midsummer's Day,' he concluded, 'I will have reached the ripe old age of a hundred and four.' Sadly, Arthur Tomkins fell in his house on the day I had arranged to visit him and died in hospital a few days after his birthday.

My special thanks to Dominick Browne (aka Lord Mereworth) for the trouble he took in furnishing me with interesting snippets of information about his late father Lord Oranmore and Browne. The tour of Luggala that he arranged for my benefit was especially rewarding and I would like to thank the current owner, the Honourable Garech Browne, and the staff Mary O'Leary, Noleen Webster and Nicholas Myers – for their hospitality.

Thanks to Richard Hamilton for photographs of the crash scene taken by his mother, Hilary, and for his own interest in the story.

In St Bricin's Hospital Lieutenant Colonel Browne was extremely helpful and kindly gave me a tour of Ward One. I was also able to see some of the medical notes from 1946, still filed in his office. Colonel Laffan, a medical orderly in St Bricin's Hospital at the time, showed me his diary entries for 1946 and gave me much useful information on Ireland during the Emergency.

I am very grateful to all the staff of the National Library, Pearse Street Library, Kevin Street Library and Bray Library, where I spent many hours poring over books, newspapers and articles. Particular thanks to Robert Butler for his help and enthusiasm.

Thanks to the staff of the National Archives in Dublin, to Pat Magee of An Garda Síochána Archives in the Phoenix Park and to the staff of the Irish Military Archives.

I would also like to acknowledge the contributions made by the late Charlie Keegan and the late Moira Cooke.

Stephane Casteran and Gwendal Sousset of the French Embassy in Dublin pointed me in the direction of much French archive material. Dominique Havard of the Association des Amis Archives Diplomatiques in Nantes was extremely helpful and gave permission to use photographs held in the archives. The graphic photos serve to define the moment more than words could ever do. The staff of the Archives de l'Armée de l'Air provided useful archive material and information on the aircraft involved.

In England, I would like to thank Margaret Courtney of the UK Girl Guides for her help in accessing relevant material in their well-documented archives and thank also the staff of the Coombes Croft Library in Tottenham, London.

I owe a special thanks to Michael Dowling, who walked the Wicklow Way in 2002 and was the first person to tell me about the incident, after reading an intriguing entry in his guidebook.

For trekking tirelessly with me in the Wicklow Mountains in all weathers and for learning to make a half-decent soup, I am indebted to Paddi Slater, whom I also dragged uncomplainingly to off-the-beaten-track areas of Paris such as Drancy and Le Bourget.

Thanks to Brendan Quinn for his enthusiasm and suggestions regarding the structure of the book. I am very grateful to him for keeping me on track and for being so brutally honest in his appraisal of my first draft, even if I didn't appreciate it at the time.

I would specially like to thank Lauren Byrne for her incisive comments and helpful suggestions. Thanks also to Colm Gallagher, Billy Doran and Jane Berry for useful comments and encouragement, and particularly to Billy for information on the will-o'-the-wisp.

Many thanks to all the staff at New Island, especially to Emma Dunne who meticulously edited the book and was refreshingly honest in her appraisal. Fidelma Slattery spent many hours designing the cover of the book with stunnning results. Joseph Hoban, as always, put his multifaceted skills to brilliant use in marketing the book. Deirdre Nolan made intelligent suggestions. Thanks to Christina Ramminger and Alistair Verschoyle for selling the book. I am grateful to Conor Graham and Michael Darcy for effortlessly taking over many of the responsibilities of my 'day job'. And when all appeared to be lost Steffen Higel, with technical wizardry, stepped in and revived my computer.

For assuaging my doubts and fears about the validity of this project, I am most grateful to John Laher, Kevin Halliwell, Keith Johnson, Tony Talbot, Jane Talbot, Jenny Talbot, Peter Barnes and, last but not least, my publisher Edwin Higel who, in a Baggot Street restaurant some time in February 2003, originally broached the subject of a book.

Lilette Lemoine and Chantal Lacoin went to enormous trouble to put me in touch with other French Guides from this period and reliably followed up on my numerous queries. For the warm reception I received in France, my heartfelt thanks go to all the French Guides of 1946. I little imagined when I first took, with some trepidation, the lift to Lilette's fifth-floor apartment in the sixteenth *arrondissement* of Paris in May 2003 that I would be embarking on what would prove to be a major but stimulating challenge. Their extraordinary vigour and enthusiasm for this project have been an inspiration to me in writing their story.

I would like to express my deepest thanks to Chantal Lacoin (*née* de Vitry), Lilette Lemoine (*née* Levy-Bruhl), Andrée Brocard (*née* Bonnet), Nicole Lucquin (*née* Jacques-Léon), Antoinette Grandguillot (*née* Emo), Antoinette Roudot (*née* Nattier), Catherine Bertier (*née* de Geuser), Jacqueline Plottin (*née* Conort), Geneviève Carrière (*née* Bétrancourt), Agnès Vallin (*née* Laporte), Janine Fistel (*née* Alexandre), Françoise Béchet, Ginette Rogier (*née* Martin), Anne Parez (*née* Lemonnier), Eliane Royer (*née* Lemonnier), Magali Petitmengin (*née* Noyer), Monique Divetain (*née* Ygouf), Odile Longour (*née* Lecoquière), Micheline Huré (*née* Bourdeauducq) and to the memory of Odile Stahlberger and *la Benjamine* Sylvia Ostrowetsky, to all of whom – *les rescapées* – I humbly dedicate this book.

Prologue

The plane juddered, buffeted by a sudden clash of air currents. The ladies exchanged anxious glances. And then they all laughed, diffusing the tension in an instant.

Aer Lingus flight EI525 was commencing its descent into Dublin Airport. On board, a party of French ladies talked with much exuberance, as they had done throughout their journey from Paris.

Although they displayed a certain politeness towards each other, such as strangers might do, there was a bond between these older women forged by more than just a common language. Their conversation was expansive, filled with children and houses, details of lives well lived. Yet at times they behaved like girls again, in a way only they could understand. As the sea and low hills loomed larger, one or two of them craned their necks for a better view of the brown domes below, toy-like and two-dimensional from the air.

Removing a red and blue cotton scarf from her bag, Madame Lacoin, the leader of the party, tied it loosely around her neck. As if in tune, the others followed suit with scarves of the same design. Everyone was smiling and an air of expectancy suffused the cabin.

In Dublin, everything had been arranged. Photographers and journalists were standing by at the airport. A bus had been hired to take the ladies to Enniskerry, where they would have a light lunch in Powerscourt Gardens. On Sunday, those who wished would attend a special mass in the Catholic church and later there would be some entertainment: Irish dancing in the Guide cottage in Enniskerry where, eschewing the luxury of a hotel, they would stay in the Bunk Room. The simplicity of the Bunk Room was perfectly suited to their purpose – for they were pilgrims not tourists – and although they planned to look at the *Book of Kells* in Trinity College and visit the Kilkenny Design shop on Nassau Street, they would be following a very different itinerary to those suggested by Bord Fáilte.

The welcoming committee was anxious that this should be as happy an occasion as possible and they were waiting at the airport in quiet anticipation.

As the fuselage continued to vibrate in the mild turbulence, one of the women leant over to a young man sitting next to her. He was fidgety: one moment scratching his forehead, the next gripping the armrests with cold, clammy hands. 'You know,' she said, gently touching his arm, 'they don't usually drop out of the sky. You'll be fine with me.'

On a dismal day in August 1946 the *Indian Reefer* docked at Dublin's quays with 60,000 cases of Brazilian oranges from Rio de Janeiro. The SS *Penestin* left Dublin for Le Havre, carrying three tons of turf briquettes bound for the Irish Red Cross hospital in the small Normandy town of Saint Lô. One thousand one hundred passengers stepped off the mail boat at Dun Laoghaire, which had rolled heavily on its journey from Holyhead. The ship had been full to capacity.

That same month, one week after the Dublin Horse

Show, the owner of a small hotel in County Wicklow opened the door to a young woman drenched to the bone. Beyond the threshold, a flame flickered up for a moment in the hearth. Four hours later, seven miles away, two dark shapes moved across a lawn next to a lake. The figures stumbled past a lighted window, the curtains billowing on a gust of wind.

Nine hundred and fifty horses, the biggest entry since 1914, had participated in the Dublin Horse Show that year, the first since 1939. It had been delightful to see the French back in the ring again.

France had been in a state of catalepsy for the past seven years and was just beginning to come alive again. It was only a year since the hostilities in Europe had ended, a war that had wreaked chaos across the country. Paris had experienced fifty months of enemy occupation and two appalling post-liberation winters. Whole swaths of the country, particularly in the north, had been completely destroyed. The people were starting to relish their freedom again and they were bursting with energy – energy that had been pent up for more than four years of occupation and two of liberation.

What people needed was a complete change of scene and some good, wholesome food. Many were keen to travel abroad again but demand was so great that there were hardly any seats available by sea until the end of September and virtually no passengers could be taken by air until October. People were being advised to delay any travel unless it was absolutely essential.

When a group of French Girl Guides was given the opportunity to travel free to Ireland by aeroplane, it sounded like the chance of a lifetime.

Part 1

Question: Guides, Eclaireuses — Toujours?
Réponse: Prêtes.

One

'Our thoughts and sympathies are with those other Guides who are suffering such hardships in lands less fortunate than our own. We can only hope and pray for happier times and remember the contacts with our sister Guides in many lands, made in that spirit of friendship which, through all the isolation of war time conditions, unites us through the Guide movement.'

Ethel Moore, International Commissioner of The Irish
Girl Guides, 1939

On the seventh Sunday after Easter in 1946, Margaret Hamilton-Reid, a lieutenant in Rathfarnham Rangers, made her first trip to France with Ethel Moore, the International Commissioner of The Irish Girl Guides, and Mrs Lillis, the Area Commissioner for Dublin.

Travel to international camps and conferences had been halted during the war. The last gathering, Pax Ting – a curious title drawn from different languages, which roughly translated as 'friendly peace gathering' – had taken place in Hungary in August 1939 amid continuing fears of war. New friends departed saying, 'If war comes, we must keep our friendships. If we cannot meet, if we cannot write, if we never see each other again – we can remember each other and we can pray for each other.'

During the Emergency, as this period was called in Ireland, The Irish Girl Guides had written to the government offering help as a movement. They were soon called upon to assemble civilian gas masks in Dublin. Senior members were encouraged to bring their first-aid training up to date and attend air-raid precautions lectures. They collected sphagnum moss for the Irish Red Cross for use as wound dressings in hospitals. Many Guides helped in the Red Cross depots in Cork and Dublin.

Two years after the death of Lord Baden-Powell in 1941, The Irish Girl Guides decided to start a memorial fund to commemorate him, as their British counterparts were doing in the UK – at this time Guiding was very much associated with Britain. The money would be used to build a cottage in Enniskerry, County Wicklow, on land donated by the Powerscourts. (Lady Powerscourt was the first Chief Commissioner of The Irish Girl Guides.) The cottage would become a centre for outdoor Guiding.

They wanted to use part of the fund for relief work amongst the children and young women in Europe. For The Irish Girl Guides, the enterprise was an offer of support to people in need. They saw it as their duty to help others, especially having escaped the horrors of war themselves. In his last message to the Scouts and Guides, Lord Baden-Powell, or 'B.P.' as he became internationally known, had said, 'Your business in life is to be happy and to make others happy … to bring happiness into the world by making happier homes.' And this is exactly what they set out to do.

Individual members saved and worked to earn money. Guide companies and Brownie packs made joint efforts. They put on entertainments of all kinds, including sales of books, cakes, sweets and country produce. They set up white-elephant, parcel and lucky-dip stalls. They made cards, calendars and Christmas decorations. By 1945 the B.P. Memorial Fund had reached the sum of £1,950, representing sixteen shillings per head of the Guide population.

For a small movement of only about 2,500 members, their plans were quite ambitious. They managed to raise enough money to buy a van, equipped with tents and other Guiding material. The van, a grey Ford V8, would represent The Irish Girl Guides in Europe. Named *Arethusa*, not after the nymph in classical mythology, but after the director of the World Bureau (the secretariat of the World Association of Girl Guides), its aim was to restart Guiding after the war where it had either stopped or gone underground. *Arethusa* eventually set out for Austria in 1947 with the World Flag – adopted as a symbol of the World Movement – flying above its radiator.

One year after peace was declared in Europe, the prospect of travel to the continent filled Margaret Hamilton-Reid with expectation. 'I was so excited,' she remembered. 'I was prancing around – this wild Irish girl running in circles in my Guide uniform.' She waved goodbye to her aunt, with whom she was living in Rathgar on the south side of Dublin, suffused by a sense of anticipation.

Her journey took her on the newly opened Golden Arrow train service from Victoria Station in London to the Gare du Nord. Apart from her disappointment at how grubby the White Cliffs of Dover looked, she was struck, coming into Calais, by the devastation that war had wreaked on the country. Calais had no harbour. It was in ruins. 'The French train then just rumbled along slowly towards Paris, stopping at Amiens, Reims; and everywhere was in ruins.'

When Mrs Lillis, Ethel Moore and Margaret Hamilton-Reid returned to Ireland from France, Mrs Lillis proposed that a party of French and Dutch Guides should be invited to spend a three-week holiday in Ireland during the summer.

She and other Leaders felt that what these children needed most of all, after years of nervous strain, fatigue and privation, was a good holiday, complete rest and some nourishing Irish food.

The Irish Girl Guides contacted the Department of External Affairs, and St Columba's College, the boys' school in Rathfarnham on the outskirts of Dublin, was put at their disposal. Mrs Lillis decided to use £200 from the B.P. Memorial Fund to finance the Dutch and French visit. They had about two months to put their plans into action.

Mrs Lillis and Eileen Beatty, Secretary of The Irish Girl Guides, made all the arrangements. It was left to the national movements in each country to select who should come. They decided that the French and Dutch girls would be allowed to sleep in dormitories at St Columba's College. After years of hardship, they felt that the girls' health had probably suffered – and so it was to prove. The stronger Irish Guides would sleep outside under canvas.

The original plan was for the girls from both countries to travel by boat and train via London and Liverpool but at this point the French intervened.

Largely for diplomatic reasons, the French government became very interested in what Ireland was doing after the war. Margaret Hamilton-Reid remarked that, at the time, 'People were excited by the smallest things.' While being very pleased with The Irish Girl Guides' post-war gesture, the French in effect said, 'We don't want you to spend all your money; we will bring them over ourselves.' Madame de Beaulieu, conducting the negotiations for the Guides de France and Eclaireuses, informed the Irish organisers that they would provide an Armée de l'Air (French Air Force) plane, free of charge, and a young French crew to transport the girls to Ireland.

In the meantime, the Dutch party would travel by boat and train as arranged.

Scoutisme Français 1946

Scoutisme Français is an organisation consisting of all the Guide and Scout movements in France: the Eclaireurs et Eclaireuses, the Scouts de France and the Guides de France.

The Guides de France is a feminine, Catholic Scouting association open to all. The Eclaireuses is a feminine association open to all religions without distinction.

AGE GROUPS

Guides de France/Eclaireuses	*Girl Guides*
8–11 Jeannettes/Louvettes	Brownies
11–17 Guides/Eclaireuses	Girl Guides/Girl Scouts
17–20 Aînées	Rangers
20+ Cheftaines	Leaders

RANKS

French	*English/Irish*
Commissaire	Commissioner
Cheftaine	Guider/Leader/Captain
Chef d'Equipe	Patrol Leader

Two

Mademoiselle Chantal de Vitry was on holiday near the village of Barbentane, where the great rivers of the Rhône and the Durance converged, when she received a telephone call out of the blue. Shortly afterwards, she was standing at the station in Avignon, waiting for the next train to Paris.

Madame de Beaulieu, the International Commissioner of the Guides de France, explained that there had been a last-minute emergency in her plans to send a group of Guides de France and Eclaireuses to a holiday camp in Ireland.

The Cheftaine, the leader of the party, would be unavoidably detained in France. Her son had been rushed to hospital with appendicitis and she was unable to leave his bedside. All arrangements had been made and the French government had been kind enough to provide an aeroplane to transport everybody free of charge. The trip could not be delayed.

The International Commissioner's question, which had the authority of a summons, was simple. Would Chantal, an experienced Guider who had participated in many summer camps in France, step in as the new Cheftaine?

They were leaving in two days' time.

Chantal was excited at the idea of travelling abroad and delighted at the prospect of going by aeroplane for the first time in her life. As the eldest of ten children, she was used to taking on responsibilities. Without hesitation she agreed to take the next train back to Paris, leaving her family to continue their holiday in the South of France.

Surrounded by the rhythmic drone of cicadas and the scent of lavender, with the sun hot on the platform, the twenty-one-year-old Cheftaine boarded her train. As the train wound its way across the countryside, beginning its twelve-hour journey to the Gare de Lyon, the sky was an intense blue and the Provençal light, beloved by artists, gave the acres of green vines on the Luberon hills an iridescent glow.

At six o'clock on the evening of 11 August 1946, Chantal de Vitry and Andrée Bonnet, another Guides de France Cheftaine, walked down the avenue Victor Hugo. In the bustling cafés, with their new orange awnings, people were sipping *pastis* and aperitifs after walking in the park. The warm breeze, rustling through the trees, pressed against their faces. Chantal wore the yellow cravat of the 75th Paris Company; Andrée a loosely tied red cravat from her own company in Issoire, her curly dark hair pinned back in a fashionable style called *à l'aiglon*.

There was an air of vigour and activity about Paris and this spilled over to the two trim young women. They passed parents pushing baby carriages, which during the occupation had been used only for the transport of logs and turnips. Men, women, boys and girls were laughing in the street and the velvety warmth of the August evening enveloped everyone as the two Cheftaines arrived at 26 avenue Victor Hugo, the home of the International Commissioner, Madame de Beaulieu.

Twenty-year-old Andrée Bonnet had travelled to Paris by

train from Issoire in the Puy de Dôme *département,* her rucksack tightly filled with extra clothes. Once in Ireland, she was planning to extend her visit and work as a governess with an Irish family for at least two months. Chantal had invited her to stay the night at her home in the avenue Victor Hugo, the same street where Madame de Beaulieu lived. Andrée, who had not met Chantal before, was grateful to be spared the expense of a hotel. Her recently widowed mother would have found it difficult to scrape together the necessary money for an overnight stay. Apart from this, Paris was hosting the first post-war peace conference and there was hardly a hotel room to be had in the city.

In the International Commissioner's sitting-room, small groups of girls of a similar age had congregated, whispering and chattering on the eve of their trip to Ireland. From the *villes martyres* in Normandy there were thirteen Guides de France.

Normandy's thousand-year heritage perished forever during the war and the *villes martyres* were those towns that had suffered most, either under the German occupation or during the ferocious Allied bombings after D-Day, called *le jour J* in French. When liberation eventually came in 1944, the price was high. The D-Day landings claimed the lives of an estimated twenty thousand French civilians in Normandy alone. Towns such as Caen, Saint Lô and Le Havre were subsequently reduced to smoking ruins.

Five of the girls — Jacqueline Conort, Antoinette Emo, Catherine de Geuser, Agnès Laporte and Odile Lecoquière — belonged to the 2nd Le Havre Company, in the centre of the town. Geneviève Bétrancourt was the only girl from the 3rd Le Havre Company, in nearby Sainte Adresse, although she knew Agnès and Antoinette Emo through their shared Guiding activities. The girls from Le Havre clustered in one corner of the room.

A few kilometres inland from Le Havre, the town of Yvetot was the home of Anne Lemonnier and Odile Stahlberger. Close to the so-called 'Cigarette Camps', which had served as staging-area camps for the Allies before securing Le Havre, the town had been constantly under threat of attack during the war. Anne knew some of the girls from Le Havre and later she would come to depend on them in a way she could not have imagined.

Avranches, bombed by the American Air Force in June 1944, was another town strategically positioned on the coast and thus always vulnerable. From the nearby village of Le Val Saint Père, Françoise Béchet recalled how everyone had to 'measure their words' during the occupation, when discretion, even between friends, had been the order of the day. At eighteen, Françoise was the eldest of the Guides de France and well on her way to becoming a Cheftaine.

Looking younger than her sixteen years, Janine Alexandre, a timid girl, was standing alone in another corner of the room. She was from Saint Lô, where the Red Cross had set up the Irish hospital after the war: the town that became known as the most heavily damaged in all France. The Paris correspondent of *The Irish Times* had reported that, with the exception of a small group of houses in one section, not a stone had been left upon a stone in this once-prosperous market town. Earlier that month, Samuel Beckett had spoken of the devastation in a broadcast on Irish radio entitled 'Capital of Ruins' and later Janine said how grateful the population of Saint Lô was to Ireland for the hospital, which in those days was the only cheering sight around.

Apart from Chantal, who had spent one summer in Lowestoft before the war, none of the girls had been out of France before. Only Françoise had ever been on an aeroplane. Travel overland was difficult enough so soon after the war, which had destroyed half of the country's infrastructure.

The girls had travelled to Paris by train across a country

that had taken on a naked and bruised look after the ravages of war. France had lost over a quarter of its wealth to war damage and this was particularly noticeable in the north and east. In February 1944, the French railways had been bombed, cutting off Normandy from the rest of the country. The Le Havre-town girls had travelled together, passing through a gutted Dieppe. Outside Rouen, a viaduct had been blown up. They had to get off one train and walk to the other side of the tracks to catch another. It wasn't something that they found unusual.

'Enjoy yourself now. We'll want to hear all about it when you get back,' Geneviève Bétrancourt's friends had said as she waved goodbye to them at the station in Le Havre. She promised that she would have plenty of stories to tell them on her return in three weeks' time.

On 10 August, Janine Alexandre stood in the newly constructed station at Saint Lô. 'I said farewell to all my little family, who were just as emotional as I was – *"la petite dernière"*, the youngest little one, was leaving her mother to go far away.'

The train rumbled out of her ruined town, on through green fields and eventually arrived on the outskirts of Paris, pulling its way past buildings covered in soot to end its journey at Saint Lazare Station, where Janine was 'gathered up' by friends and family who put her up and took her to the meeting with Madame de Beaulieu the next day.

Monique Ygouf, Eliane Lemonnier and Antoinette Nattier had travelled to Paris separately from Cherbourg, where they belonged to different companies. As the Germans' launch pad for attacking Britain, this part of northern France was littered with military bases and airfields. A V2 rocket launch pad had been installed a few metres from Eliane's home and inflatable lifeboats stood in the playground shelters of her school.

Twenty-five kilometres away, in the centre of the Cotentin Peninsular, the village of Sainte Mère Eglise, with a population of 1,500, had been noted only for breeding horses until two hours before 6 June 1944. Monique's family home was completely destroyed when the 82nd Airborne Division parachuted into her village. Her family was forced to move to nearby Valognes, where they had to start again from scratch.

Ten kilometres from Cherbourg, the pretty little town of Valognes was also Antoinette Nattier's home. An only child, she was making her first trip to Paris alone. It was a daunting experience. Nervous and bewildered she travelled up the Champs Elysées, past children enjoying donkey rides in the Tuileries, and she gazed at the Eiffel Tower for the first time in her life. In the Commissioner's sitting-room, however, it wasn't long before Geneviève Bétrancourt took her under her wing and introduced her to the girls from Le Havre.

Odile Lecoquière recalled a feeling of immense pleasure at this first meeting. She remembered how all the girls, most of whom were Chef d'Equipes (Patrol Leaders) in their companies, sat around in circles, as they would in their patrols at home, exchanging information about themselves and their families. As Guides de France, they had all made the same solemn promise:

> Sur mon honneur, avec la grâce de Dieu, je m'engage à servir de mon mieux Dieu, l'Eglise et la Patrie, à aider mon prochain en toutes circonstances à observer la Loi des Guides. [I promise on my honour to do my best to serve God, the Church and my country, to help others at all times to obey the Guide Law.]

The Guide Law was a set of precepts and was more or less the same worldwide, with only slight variations from country to country.

Like well-behaved Girl Guides, they played games to get to know each other. Their order and discipline hinted at a generation that had lived through and withstood the trials of war. War was a part of history they had become caught up in when they were just growing up. Whether strong or weak, they had all endured the privations that war and rationing had brought, as the Germans requisitioned most of France's raw materials and finished products. Though not directly involved in the hostilities, they had sat shivering in unheated classrooms as imports were cut off and oil and coal supplies dwindled to nothing. Perhaps these experiences made them more likely to understand and cope with a whole host of things that might seem impossible for teenagers now.

Agnès Laporte, Catherine de Geuser, Jacqueline Conort and Antoinette Emo had spent nights sheltering in cellars during the bombing raids on Le Havre. Geneviève Bétrancourt, Odile Lecoquière and Eliane Lemonnier had suffered the trauma of evacuation to the country to escape the expected bombings in the town. Both Catherine and Antoinette Nattier's fathers had been prisoners-of-war. Like many other families, Catherine's had billeted German officers sharing their kitchen. Antoinette Emo's cousin had died in Dachau. Her family never discussed his suffering – it simply wasn't mentioned.

Rising to their feet as the International Commissioner entered the room, the girls immediately extinguished their conversation. In their military-style navy-blue uniforms, they stood to attention and listened in silence to Madame de Beaulieu's final words of wisdom: 'You must be impeccable,' exhorted Madame de Beaulieu. 'I particularly recommend that you even polish your belts. Above all,' she paused, casting her eyes about the room, 'do not forget that you are representing France.'

Standards for Baden-Powell Girl Guides

Do you put on your uniform correctly? Is it clean and pressed and polished? Are you a really smart advertisement for our great movement?

Do you stand and walk as beautifully as you are able? Can you take your place in Company Drill in threes and march smartly and correctly?

The Tenderfoot Test is the foundation of everything in our movement. Do you really know it through and through? Can you still tie a sheet bend and hoist a flag? Do you know the secret signs and can you follow a trail? Do you think about the Law and the Promise and really try to live your life with these before you?

UK Guiding, 1946

Three

The Guides de France rose at dawn on Monday morning, 12 August 1946. With hands scrubbed, nails clean and trimmed, their neat hair was brushed and tied back from their faces. Spotless, within and without, they wore navy-blue dresses or skirts and shirts, coloured cravats, long white socks and big walking shoes. Their shoes and badges were polished. Attached to their belts were knives and whistles. Navy-blue capes and berets completed the ensemble. The long capes were an important part of a Guide's uniform, as they could double up as blankets. In their rucksacks, they carried a camp dress and neckerchief.

Janine later recalled how, at a self-conscious age, when appearance was very important, their developing coquetry and sense of style must have suffered from this quasi-military attire, faced with the elegance of other people that they passed on the streets. Despite the war, Paris was still the city of unmistakable *chic*. The draped turban, the chemise, the pleated skirt were at the cutting edge of *haute couture*. Although Coco had left France before the liberation, Maison Chanel was a house to be reckoned with. Other names such as Reboux, Schiaparelli, Lanvin and Balenciaga flourished in the capital. Most teenagers would have spent hours in front of the mirror, rehearsing for life as an adult. The Guides de France were turned out with very little consideration for fashion.

For some of the girls, it had been difficult to put together even the barest essentials for the trip after the hardships of the last seven years. Odile Lecoquière had to borrow everything from her friends and family. Jacqueline Conort was wearing her cousin's shoes, which were uncomfortably tight. She had also borrowed a rucksack.

After breakfast at six o'clock, the Guides de France, smelling of soap and water, set out for Le Bourget Airport near Drancy on the north-east outskirts of Paris, where they would meet Lilette Levy-Bruhl and the Eclaireuses.

Paris awoke at an unearthly hour in the morning and by 6.30 A.M. the sound of ear-piercing klaxons filled the air. The city teemed with five thousand proper taxis, as that summer saw the end of the bicycle-powered *vélotaxis*. Each of the twenty-one delegations attending the peace conference had arrived with a retinue of diplomats, officials, journalists, secretaries and hangers-on, ceaselessly ferried to and fro past the cafés on the Grands Boulevards.

'I am Cheftaine de Vitry,' announced Chantal to Lilette Levy-Bruhl when they met for the first time at Le Bourget Airport. Lilette, Cheftaine of the Eclaireuses, thought she was referring to Vitry, a working-class suburb or *banlieue* on the outskirts of Paris.

Lilette, with thick brown hair and a dark complexion, wore a white blouse and chestnut-brown skirt, the uniform of the Eclaireuses. Like Chantal and Andrée, she had not met any of the girls before. An article had appeared in *l'Alouette*, the Eclaireuse magazine, mentioning the possibility of a summer camp in Ireland and Lilette had applied. At twenty-two, she had participated in a few summer camps in France but she had never been abroad or travelled by plane before.

Unlike the Guides de France, who were all from Normandy, the Eclaireuses had travelled to Le Bourget from different parts of France.

From the small Brittany port of Nantes, a town where 1,500 bombs were dropped in 1943, Ginette Martin had arrived in Paris by train, her first time travelling alone. She was nervous but excited. She wore a new uniform and carried a rucksack on her back, bought specially for the camp in Ireland. She was proud to be the only girl selected from her Protestant company, but she waved goodbye to a tearful mother.

When all clothes were rationed, it was a great privilege to be able to buy a new uniform. Ginette was lucky. Magali Noyer, who belonged to the Eclaireuses Unionistes de France, a Protestant company in Paris, had also been given a voucher to purchase a new uniform for the trip. Her neat brown skirt and pullover, of which she was inordinately proud, were the envy of all her friends.

Although Paris was liberated in 1944, it took a long time for life to return to anything approaching normality. Most staples were rationed. Two years after the liberation of Paris, the average citizen received less than seven ounces of fat a week and little more than half a pound of meat. Eighteen-year-old Micheline Bourdeauducq came from Vincennes on the eastern limits of Paris. Like the rest of the capital, this suburb had escaped serious damage during the war but food was always a struggle to come by. The severe shortages meant that Micheline's mother often paid vastly inflated prices to buy food from the country. When the average monthly wage was 2,300 francs, butter on the flourishing black market was 1,000 francs a kilo. Otherwise, she waited for hours, sometimes during the night, to be among the first in the queue when a shop opened.

After the fall of France in 1940, when many families left the capital for the *zone libre*, the unoccupied southern part of France, food was always in short supply. Chantal de Vitry's father had moved his manufacturing business to an area near Avignon at this time. Chickpeas and swedes, traditionally despised and grown only for cattle fodder, became a staple in the de Vitry kitchen as their store cupboards became virtually empty.

The promise of more to eat was one of the attractions of Scouting for Nicole Jacques-Léon, from Grenoble, during the war. Participation in camps organised by her local Eclaireuse company always meant that she received a little extra food.

As the enthusiastic fourteen-year-old Nicole had waited for the train to Paris with her mother, sister and envious little brother Daniel, she had not felt the least bit nervous. Paris was a city that she had spent the early part of her life in – until the Germans had arrived. Her family had then fled to Grenoble, which became part of the Italian Zone – a small section of French territory west of the Alps where a benign Italian administration provided a haven for Jewish families, such as Nicole's. A confident, bespectacled girl, she had attended many summer camps and knew all the camp songs. On arriving at the airport, Nicole mingled easily with the rest of the Guides and Eclaireuses.

The other girls, however, were harbouring a mixture of emotions. A certain amount of anxiety and reserve was tempered by curiosity and obvious excitement at the prospect of meeting new friends from France, Ireland and Holland. Their Cheftaines and parents had stressed how lucky they were to have been chosen for the trip. Nevertheless, fourteen-year-old Catherine de Geuser from Le Havre had mixed feelings. She was nervous of travelling abroad for the first time and she was worried that she did not speak English. For her the trip was something to be endured rather than enjoyed.

Françoise Béchet and Janine Alexandre, alert to portents, also had an uneasy feeling, a sense of foreboding, which did not find expression in words.

Earlier in the month Janine, like the other Guides and Eclaireuses, had received a letter dated 2 August, signed by the International Commissioner, confirming the arrangements for their departure on 12 August.

'It is a great honour to represent the Guides de France,' wrote Madame de Beaulieu. 'I count on you to exercise this task with tact, delicacy and distinction.'

Although Janine found this remark intimidating enough for a young teenager about to leave her family for the first time, it was not these words that had provoked such a bad feeling. 'No, it was rather the more prosaic: "You have the opportunity to travel free by AEROPLANE on 12 August."

'By aeroplane! I was not a particularly nervous person. Premonition or not, I was physically shocked.' Everything from then on, in retrospect, was a signpost pointing towards calamity.

At the time, though, this ominous feeling was quickly eclipsed by the pride and pleasure she felt at being selected. 'I was going to take a plane, leave France for the first time – marvellous.'

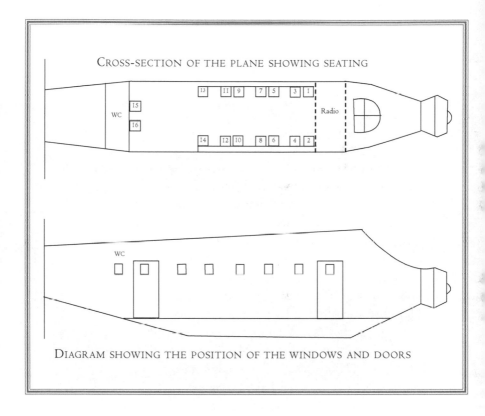

CROSS-SECTION OF THE PLANE SHOWING SEATING

DIAGRAM SHOWING THE POSITION OF THE WINDOWS AND DOORS

Four

～～～

At Le Bourget Airport, 'the silver plane was glittering in the early morning sun', recalled Lilette. The girls had no sense that there was anything unusual about the military aircraft waiting to transport them to Ireland. It was just after the war and, therefore, quite common to see this type of aeroplane. The important thing was that they were going to Dublin.

The Junkers Ju-52/3M, with its huge wingspan and three engines, sat solidly on the ground, displaying a red, white and blue disc surrounded by a band of yellow – the insignia of the Armée de l'Air. A large letter B was emblazoned on its big, high tail with the code 046. The nose was painted with the sign: '*Groupe Maine*'. Below this was a blue crest, red-bordered, with a golden fleur-de-lis.

The plane, fondly nicknamed *Tante Ju* (Auntie Ju), made little concession to beauty. Pieces stuck out of the airframe and corrugated sheets of metal covered the surface of the machine – including the wings, which were fixed by giant cables to the fuselage. The legs of the landing gear were equipped with shock absorbers, making it possible to land on unstable ground on its great big wheels. The trademark corrugated alloy skin created a much sturdier machine than those made from metal tubes or fabric but, as a result, it had the reputation of being heavier and slower than other aircraft of the time.

The original one-engine prototype was designed by Hugo Junkers, a pioneer of air transport and a name synonymous with the construction of reliable, high-performance planes.

The Ju-52s, built by the German airline Lufthansa in 1932, were originally designed as passenger airliners but later became the workhorse of the Luftwaffe during the war, flying the Nazi colours and performing all sorts of missions from troop transport to mine laying. For fifteen years they were the symbol of German aviation. During the occupation of France, the Germans signed an agreement with the French authorities to construct 321 planes in the former Amiot factories in Colombes in the suburbs of Paris.

The French aeronautical industry was destroyed during the war but afterwards the former German planes were put back into use by the Armée de l'Air, as part of the war reparations, at the Amiot factory, now called the Ateliers Aéronautiques de Colombes. The factory started to produce Ju-52s under the name AAC.1 Toucan. The French army and navy used the Toucans for the transport of paratroopers, for bomber missions and as military ambulances. In 1946, once again *Tante Ju* was put to use to carry civilians.

At Le Bourget, the Guides de France and Eclaireuses lined up in front of their leaders, as Chantal, holding a collective passport for all of the girls, ticked their names off her list.

Before boarding the aircraft, however, the girls themselves had to be weighed. Their bulging rucksacks were also put on the scales. Even though they had only the basic necessities for a three-week camping holiday – a camping dress, a knife, a spoon, a fork, a bathing costume and a few personal items –

the girls were told to lighten their load. Nevertheless, Françoise held on to her prayer book. Ginette and the girls from Le Havre kept their cameras. Janine and Monique clung to their pencils and little blank notebooks.

One of the last to board, Lilette, who was in her own words 'a well-built girl', feared that she might not be allowed onto the plane, which was already filled to capacity. Would her weight tip the scales? She recalled an argument with the ground staff. This was not, however, on her account. With no available seats on any of the scheduled flights that day, a man was pleading with the authorities to let him board the Junkers plane but for all his gesticulating he was not permitted onto the aircraft. Later, Lilette often wondered about this man: how he felt and if he considered himself a son of fortune in the end.

'We climbed into the plane in reverse alphabetical order: Ygouf, Stahlberger, Noyer, Nattier, Martin,' recalled Geneviève Bétrancourt, 'but afterwards everybody swapped around.'

'When we got on the plane, we found a row of small individual folding seats, made of tubular metal, facing each other,' observed Antoinette Nattier, a flat cushion the only concession to comfort. Antoinette was second after the cockpit, on the right next to Geneviève Bétrancourt, whom she had befriended the evening before at the International Commissioner's house.

'It was narrow and uncomfortable,' remarked Janine. 'Militaire quoi?' The plane was adapted for carrying troops, with typically military-style narrow, removable bench seats running the length of the cabin.

The girls were thus sitting opposite each other with their knees touching, their rucksacks wedged underneath the seats.

Cramped and uncomfortable as it was for those with a seat, the plane was designed to carry only sixteen passengers. Chantal, therefore, was faced with trying to squeeze the remaining Guides into the already overcrowded cabin.

Four of the girls were obliged to squat on the floor. Odile Lecoquière, still beaming with the thrill of it all, did not mind this discomfort at all. Antoinette Emo made herself as comfortable as possible at her companions' feet. Propping her navy-blue beret on the fire extinguisher, Françoise was happier to crouch at this level, 'at the back, leaning against the door', where she felt safer.

Through a little panel at the front of the cabin, Jacqueline could see the wireless operator, Daniel Duran. He wore a short-peaked cap, a battle jacket and blue trousers: the uniform of the Armée de l'Air. In the cockpit, the navigator was checking the aerial maps on which he would plot the track of the plane. The pilot was talking to the meteorological officers at Le Bourget, updating his weather report for the journey. The flight engineer was checking the instruments. Only the air hostess came into the cabin to talk to the girls.

The young crew of five was under the charge of the pilot, Capitaine Christian Habez. At twenty-nine, he had the good looks of a matinée idol. Trained in Marrakech, he had been in the Armée de l'Air since 1937. An experienced pilot, he was also an excellent navigator.

During the war, he had made the trip across the Channel and served with the British Air Force bomber squadron stationed in Yorkshire. With over 250 hours of flying experience on this type of aircraft, he was considered one of the best pilots in Le Bourget.

The second in command was Aspirant Michel Tourret, the co-pilot and navigator. They were assisted by Adjutant Daniel Duran, the wireless operator, and by flight engineer Georges Biagioni. The fifth member of the crew was the air hostess, Antoinette de Brimont, who, like the pilot, was also twenty-nine.

It was reported in the newspapers that the plane had been

on a mission to Ireland earlier in the year, transporting a consignment of strawberries from the south of France to Dublin, but none of the crew had flown to Ireland before and they were probably not familiar with the landscape. It is unlikely that they knew much about the vagaries of the Irish weather either, which swept in from the Atlantic with few checks on its progress.

In the cabin, Geneviève took out her old Kodak camera and clicked. The shot would be the only photograph to be taken of the girls before the flight. It is an animated picture – and one that they would treasure for the rest of their lives. On the far right, Andrée Bonnet stands to attention. Next to her sits Anne Lemonnier beaming into the camera, her fair, curled hair gripped back under her beret, her eyes sparkling. Squeezed between Anne and a radiant Catherine is Agnès, momentarily caught with her head turned away from the lens. Out of focus, towards the back, Jacqueline, her cape tied over her shoulders, cranes her neck above Antoinette Emo, a dark-haired girl with glasses hunched up on the floor. On the left of the picture, Chantal smiles into the camera, clutching the red and yellow banner of the 75th Paris Company, the banner that will be held high at the Irish camp by the Guides de France. Janine Alexandre peeks over her shoulder. On Chantal's other side, the Cheftaine of the Eclaireuses, Lilette, looks straight ahead, a resolute expression on her face.

As the two Cheftaines chatted on the plane, Lilette soon discovered that Chantal de Vitry was not from the *banlieue* after all but belonged to an old, respected family that had lived in the avenue Victor Hugo for many years. The de Vitry's house in the sixteenth *arrondissement* was only a few streets away from Lilette's own family apartment, amongst the many elegant flats, houses and mansions that led up to the Bois de Boulogne.

The misunderstanding gave them some amusement and soon Lilette was telling Chantal about her own name. The Levy-Bruhls, like Chantal's family, had been among the more than two million families who had left the city as the enemy line advanced towards Paris. They had vacated their apartment in the rue Raffet in 1939 and gone to live with Lilette's grandmother in Saint Malo on the Brittany coast. However, in 1942, when the Germans occupied the whole of France, the fear of anti-Semitism increased. Even though the Levy-Bruhls were only nominally Jewish, they were forced to change their name to Brune and seek refuge in a town near Toulouse. Unlike Chantal's family, who returned to the avenue Victor Hugo in 1942, the Brunes/Levy-Bruhls only came back after the liberation of Paris in 1944. Lilette's ambition had been to become a doctor but the war had ended that dream. Instead she had studied mathematics at the University of Toulouse. Chantal was also studying mathematics, at the Sorbonne.

As the final checks were made on the plane before departure, it didn't take complex mathematics to work out someone was missing from Chantal's list.

Now everyone was waiting for the final member of their group to arrive. A small girl came tearing towards the plane like an excited child to a party.

The last of the Eclaireuses, Sylvia Ostrowetsky, arrived panting at the door. She was thirteen years old but looked even younger and became known as *la Benjamine* (the youngest one). Even though she had one of the shortest journeys to make, from the suburbs of Paris, she was late. 'I was racing to catch *this* plane.'

Sylvia belonged to one of only two Jewish families in the suburb of Gentilly, on the outskirts of Paris (the name, ironically, meant town of the Gentiles). She had joined the Eclaireuses the year before the trip. Her half-illiterate father, *un chiffonier* (a rag-and-bone man), had emigrated from Poland to Paris in 1923 – 'with five francs in his pocket' – and arrived in the rue des Rosiers, near the Saint Paul métro station, expecting to be safe in France, a country priding itself on being a land of refuge. According to Sylvia, her father was always running: first from Poland and then in France, when the family was forced to flee to the *zone libre* in 1942.

Sylvia threw herself down on the metal floor of the plane near to Chantal. She looked around at the other girls and immediately felt different. Sylvia was wearing a shabby, make-do sort of uniform that her mother had cobbled together at the last minute. Her shoes were worn, her white shirt frayed at the cuffs. It was not the first time Sylvia had felt self-conscious.

At the age of eight, she had been forced to wear the Yellow Star, a piece of cloth the size of a small hand, sewn on to her clothing with the word *JUIF* printed across it in black letters. The star was meant not just to identify Jews but also to humiliate them. Not surprisingly, Sylvia felt she stood out. She had been made to feel ashamed during the war, she had been branded a 'dirty Jew', and that shame always hung remotely over her childhood.

Chantal and Lilette welcomed her aboard. Soon she was talking to everybody and completely forgot about her appearance. It was exhilarating. She was going on a trip to Dublin. The holiday feeling infected all the other girls in the cabin.

Thirty seconds later the air hostess, Antoinette de Brimont, clamped shut the big metal door of the plane.

Five

At two minutes past nine, 8.02 GMT, the Junkers plane, carrying its twenty-one young passengers and 249 gallons of petrol, prepared to leave Le Bourget Airport near Paris. The three big BMW engines roared into action and the propellers spun at an incredible speed. Six minutes later, the pilot received clearance for Dublin.

By all accounts, this was going to be another typical summer's day, another oppressive, heat-deadening day in France's overcrowded capital. The plane was heading for Dublin – a city ten times smaller than Paris – and the verdant fields of Ireland.

In Dublin, by contrast, it was turning out to be a foul day. People woke in the morning thinking it couldn't be time to get up. It took some courage even to go out. All they could hear was the endless sound of unwanted water, seeping everywhere.

A storm had raged all through the night of Sunday 11 August and showed no sign of abating as Monday morning dawned. Dubliners donned all the waterproof clothing they could find as the city streets began to resemble mini rivers. Bus queues mushroomed on the crowded pavements.

In the Country Shop, Moira Cooke, a commanding

officer at the Rathfarnham camp, was organising a reception for the French girls. Located in a basement on the north side of St Stephen's Green, the Country Shop was a popular meeting-place for lunch and tea, a place where women could display and sell rural crafts. The Irish Girl Guides often had executive meetings there, as it was round the corner from their headquarters in South Frederick Street.

Nearby, on the other side of St Stephen's Green, a tram had suddenly caught fire. The *Irish Press* reported that a continuous short circuit in the chassis had caused the apparent spontaneous combustion of the tram, a result of the 'fearful storm' that Moira Cooke would never forget.

From Dublin to the midlands, across Tipperary, Cork, Kilkenny and Limerick, bad weather enveloped the country. Fifty-mile-an-hour winds whipped up monumental seas around the coast and the gales were accompanied by torrential rain. More rain fell in one day than would normally fall in the entire month of August. It was one of the wettest days of the year. The rainfall registered at Rathfarnham was 6.89 inches.

There had been rain every day since 27 July and, as week followed week of wetness and wind, people were beginning to ask themselves if wars or atom bombs had something to do with the persistent vileness of the weather – and why were the forecasts so inaccurate? The stock reply, of course, was that Ireland was one of the most difficult places to prophesy the weather, which was determined by the movement of depressions sweeping in from the west that then often ran amok.

Holidaymakers were deluged in seaside areas and many campers, forced to flee their tents, hurried to the towns in search of accommodation, which in most cases was not available. The rough conditions prevented the departure of the French and Swedish riders and horses that had attended the Dublin Horse Show. The unloading of the *Thelma*'s cargo of timber, poles and plywood from Finland was suspended at Dublin's quays. Flooding was reported at Anglesea Bridge, Donnybrook, Clonskeagh, Ringsend and Drumcondra.

At Ailesbury Road in Dublin, Minister to France Jean Rivière and his wife were packing as the rain thrummed against the windowpanes of the French Legation. In a week's time they would be leaving Ireland for good. Monsieur Rivière was being posted to Amsterdam as the new ambassador to Holland.

Further out of the city, eleven families in Dundrum were evacuated when the Dodder burst its banks. The River Dargle overflowed into a residential area of Bray.

The severity of the storm was unprecedented in County Wicklow and damage was widespread. When the valve operator at the Vartry Reservoir near Roundwood took his measurements at nine o'clock, nearly six inches of rain had fallen in twenty-four hours. It was the worst storm that many could remember in Greystones. The Wicklow County lawn-tennis championships were postponed.

Entire hay crops were destroyed around the country and 1946 became known as 'the year of the bad harvest', recalled Brian Hogan from the Mount Maulin Hotel in Bahana near Enniskerry.

Two miles away, in Ballinagee, Charlie Keegan, son of the farmer Norman, spent much of the day sheltering from the rain as the wind tore through his cattle shed. Scythes, rakes and pitchforks leant dripping against an outhouse wall. Four cows stood forlornly in the mud outside, their tails thrashing.

There was no shelter for the council workers of County Wicklow, however. Out on the bog near the Sally Gap, Pat O'Brien dug his shovel into the sodden earth and stacked the turf into piles. Nearby, Sean Woodcock watched showers of rock spring up from the earth and fall again like grey fountains as he blasted stone in the quarry works.

Undeterred by the filthy weather, Patrick Brennan, always known as 'Pa', set out from his home in Roundwood at six-thirty in the morning with a haversack slung on his back and a belt full of cartridges. He had never missed the opening of the grouse season in his life.

At Luggala, the shooting lodge of Lord and Lady Oranmore and Browne, however, there was no shooting party that day. There were no men in plus-fours and rubber boots preparing for a day of sport on the seven-thousand-acre estate, no beaters in flat caps preparing the ground. The children were confined to the house, which nestled in the dark valley next to Lough Tay. The skin of the lake was wrinkled by the wind. The best the children could hope for was that the chauffeur would give them a lift to see the *Count of Monte Cristo* or *Tarzan Triumphs* at the cinema in Bray.

Further down the coast near Brittas Bay, a few miles south of Wicklow town, forty-six-year-old Arthur Tomkins from Dublin was spending a few days' holiday with his wife and two children at a spot commonly known as 'Jack's Hole'. He recalled that the 'morning broke cool with a heavy mist'. The mist was thicker higher up and he was waiting patiently for the sun to come and dispel it.

The Oblate Fathers Rev. O'Doherty and Rev. Keohane were reading their office in the old reformatory at Glencree and a special prayer for fine weather, *Ad Postulandam Serenitatem*, was being added to prayers at mass from Dublin to Cork. The reformatory was now being used as a temporary refugee centre, under the auspices of the Irish Red Cross. The French Sisters of Charity looked after thousands of war orphans in this building, which was once one of the barracks along the Military Road, the road built after 1798 that ran from Rathfarnham through the Sally Gap to Aughavanagh.

Driving from Wexford to Dublin, a motorist decided to take a detour through the Wicklow Mountains and the Military Road. Nine-and-a-half hours later, hours behind schedule, he arrived at his destination, hampered by water-logged roads for most of the journey. Many of the bridges were broken or had been washed away and rivers rose so quickly that they tore hedges and trees with them on their onward rush.

Stories rolled in from the provinces of damage to crops of potatoes and of wheat, oats and barley carried away by floods. North Tipperary experienced the worst rainstorm in living memory. There were tales of cattle, sheep and fat pigs being drowned and of fruit trees so denuded that one expert predicted, 'The Dublin markets will be cluttered with "windfalls" for many weeks to come.' Yachts were swamped at their moorings, trees were blown down and telephone and telegraph wires were broken.

Bill Deely, son of the local dispensary doctor in Enniskerry, later went to Prosser's Bar near the clock tower in the village – a local landmark built by the son of the fifth Lord Powerscourt to honour his father. It remains to this day a local meeting place. He was joined by his friend Conor Hogan, brother of Brian and son of the owners of the Mount Maulin Hotel near the Powerscourt Waterfall five miles away. The glittering mica schist cairn of Mount Maulin was totally obscured by the grey mist clinging to its top. It was a mist they knew all too well: its moisture soaked right through to the bone.

As the Irish Girl Guides struggled to erect their tents, it looked as if the camp in Rathfarnham was going to be a wash-out. Despite the weather, which was putting a strain on all the camp's organisers, Margaret Hamilton-Reid was looking forward to the French and Dutch visit immensely. She was eagerly awaiting the arrival of their French guests that day. The Dutch, who were travelling by boat and train, were not expected until Thursday.

She drove from Rathgar on the south side of Dublin, in her old seven-horse-power Ford (which she and her aunt had bought for £200 after the war), with her friend Eileen Beatty, the Secretary of The Irish Girl Guides, to the airport at Collinstown through roadside lakes that made waves as they trundled through them. They arrived shortly after noon, in good time to meet the French plane, which was due in an hour later.

At Dublin Airport, streaks of water trickled down the windows of the control tower. One duty officer clocked off as another signed on. The morning plane from Liverpool touched down on time at 12.03 GMT. The passengers hurried into the arrivals hall, dabbing at their necks.

Six

Capitaine Habez set his compass course for 297 degrees in accordance with the forecast for moderate south-westerly winds. The depression that had hung over Ireland, the pilot was assured by the meteorological experts in Le Bourget, would be well clear of the Irish Sea when their plane passed over.

No flight plan, departure message or indication of the flight was received at Dublin Airport.

As *Tante Ju* clattered along the runway, with no sound-proofing or insulation, the noise inside the cabin was deafening. 'We felt as if we were in a big noisy lorry,' recalled Andrée Bonnet.

Eliane Lemonnier, like Andrée, was familiar with the inside of a lorry. During the war, her college had been evacuated to Mortain, in a lower part of the Manche *département*. After D-Day, she had been forced to seek refuge in the country and it was two months before she finally managed to return to her family in Cherbourg – on a military truck.

'We were quite reassured,' said Andrée. The plane felt solid and secure.

When, for most people, flying was a novelty, the excitement of a first flight was not to be underestimated.

Some could only dream about it. 'I am told that Dublin looks so pretty from the air that pilots make a point of flying over the city to give their passengers a treat,' read a letter in *The Irish Times* on 23 September 1946.

In the *Irish Independent* on 23 August 1946, one columnist recorded his feelings:

> The great and graceful wing dashes along the ground. The grass is swirling from the rush of air. Speed is mounting. All I can see from the small window is this wing and this swept grass. I wonder where will it end.
>
> We must be near the limits of the airfield. Will she lift? – or is the pilot unable to get her off in time to clear the fences that bound the field?
>
> Just as these anxieties are reaching their climax, it becomes noticeable that the wing is a little higher over the grass and there is a decided uplift and we are in the air. There ends the first thrill of a first flight.

Despite Janine and Françoise's misgivings, *Tante Ju* lifted clear of the ground and slowly gained height, with its landing gear, which was not designed to retract, sticking straight out in the air.

As the plane soared above the calm skies of France, the girls started to relax. Jacqueline Conort, gazing out of the window at the bright clouds, soon became engrossed in the unfolding landscape below. She recognised the cliffs near her home, glinting in the sun. She could see the mouth of the Seine and she could see her demolished town of Le Havre.

Le Havre had been viciously destroyed in 1944 when the Bomber Command obliterated its centre. Jacqueline later recalled the time she had first heard about the D-Day landings, *le Débarquement* – that the Allies had arrived on the beaches of Normandy. 'On the one hand, everybody was pleased,' she said. They were going to be liberated. 'But on the other, we were nervous, not knowing if or when the Germans might seek revenge, and if they did what form the reprisals would take.' In September 1944, when Paris had already been liberated, Le Havre, which stuck out on a limb, was still in the hands of the occupiers and being pounded by shells and bombs on a daily basis.

Afterwards, Jacqueline remembered how shocked they had felt when they looked down on the port from the cliffs above the town. 'The Hôtel de Ville had completely gone. Whole swaths had gone, right up to the shore.'

The Le Havre girls could all recount some story from those terrible years – from the first *chapelet de bombes* (stick of bombs) in September 1939, when Odile Lecoquière's house had been destroyed, to the day when a housing block – *une cité* – was firebombed, burning alive all the Portuguese workers inside. It was the day Jacqueline Conort was told to put on her Holy Communion dress for the second time to follow the huge funeral cortège that made its way slowly through the town.

While Jacqueline continued to look out of the window, Normandy receded as they crossed the English Channel and the plane reached its cruising speed of 105 knots (120 miles per hour).

Janine Alexandre took out her little notebook and pencil and started to record her feelings:

> *En Avion*
>
> *Dans un nuage je note mes impressions: sensation de hauteur; de supériorité – aucune crainte.* [In a cloud, I am noting my impressions: a feeling of height; a feeling of superiority – no fear.] *Première grande aventure de ma vie.* [The first great adventure of my life.] *Nous sortons du nuage, le monde semble un jouet mignon – impression de lenteur – une heure s'écoule – nous volons sur une sorte de montagne de nuages – monotone.* [We are coming out of the cloud. The world seems like a cute little toy – impression of slowness – one hour goes by – we are flying over a mountain of clouds – boring.]

Françoise took out her own notebook and book of prayer. She was from a closely knit, deeply religious family and when

war had broken out her father, the mayor of Le Val Saint
Père, had made sure that their house, *La Nonnerie*, was
consecrated to the Sacred Heart. Shortly after the armistice
was declared, she remembered how her father had wept – *La
Nonnerie*, which locals called 'the house of the good God', had
been spared. As the plane sailed through the skies over the
Channel, Françoise buried her head in her prayer book and
put her faith in God.

With his compass course set, Capitaine Habez steered his
plane in the direction of Dublin. As he flew his plane over
Saint Valery, he observed a few clouds but his visibility, at
twenty kilometres, was good as he began to cross the English
Channel. Daniel Duran, the wireless operator, tapped out
Morse code signals every few minutes. His agile transmitting
wrist moved deftly on the Morse key as he communicated
with Le Bourget, Beauvais, Chartres and Uxbridge radio
stations. In France, the Morse operator was known as *le
pianiste*.

At 8.38 GMT Adjutant Duran tapped out a message
indicating that he was at a height of 1,500.

'Do you mean metres or feet?' returned the message from
Chartres radio station.

The language of air traffic used feet to measure height
and distance, which was more accurate than metres. The
French, however, preferred to calculate in metric measurements, which was fine within their own airspace but meant
that further afield they constantly needed to convert. The
wireless operator indicated that he was using metres.

At 8.43 the plane was at 1,800 metres and rising to 2,200
metres (7,200 feet). It is unlikely that it rose higher than this
throughout the journey. With limited de-icing equipment
and a cabin that was unpressurised, the girls were already

beginning to feel the cold. The pilot kept his machine at as low an altitude as he could. He wanted not only to see but also to be seen. At ten o'clock he flew over the Isle of Wight. At the same time he requested the call-sign and frequency of the Dublin direction finder – a Marconi-Adcock system whose mast aerials were installed in a field beside the airport.

As the cloud continued to build up in the skies over England, *Tante Ju* slowly proceeded on its course towards the south coast of Wales. The navigator, Michel Tourret, continuously examined his aerial maps and plotted the route using simple trigonometry.

As he plotted, the wind was already beginning to shift.

Seven

For the girls, the trip seemed like a big game. The aim was to reach a camp in Ireland. When they arrived at their destination they would be given more clues. They had little idea of what to expect when they arrived in the country, as they knew hardly anything about Ireland.

Sylvia had read something about the Famine. She had heard that Ireland was a poor country and that it had fought long and hard for its independence, which had also made it 'a proud country'.

They were told they would be given good, wholesome Irish food. Lilette thought this was amusing. You could then get a decent dinner of soup, a meat dish, salad and potatoes, a big dish of vegetables and a dessert for a hundred francs on the train from Paris to Toulouse. (Since the franc was devalued in December 1945, this was the equivalent of less than five shillings.) It sounded much more appetising than boiled cabbage, bacon and potatoes, which is what she had heard they ate in Ireland.

But the reality was that the average monthly income hardly allowed for a meal on the train to Toulouse. Most French citizens had to get by on their meagre rations – which nevertheless included three litres of wine per month.

Although the war years were tough for the average Irish citizen, compared with France Ireland hadn't suffered major privations during this period.

In the early days of the war, most people in the army believed it would only be a matter of time before Ireland joined in or was dragged in. There was a clear expectation that the Wehrmacht would invade both Britain and Ireland. Joseph Laffan, a member of the Irish Medical Corps at the time, recalled: 'We were afraid of invasion. If we had no army or defences, the Germans or the British could come in at any time. So we built up the army to give the impression that it wouldn't be a walk-over for them.'

Voluntary Local Defence Forces (LDFs) were established. Within twenty-four hours, representatives from every section of the community flocked in their thousands to the government's appeal. Pat O'Brien, the turf worker from Roundwood, County Wicklow, joined up, as did Lord Oranmore and Browne, the owner of the nearby shooting lodge of Luggala.

But the war never happened. The Republic of Ireland, officially called Éire, remained politically neutral throughout the Second World War and, apart from a few stray bombs, escaped the ravages and horrors that were visited on other parts of Europe during those dark years.

All major goods were rationed during the Emergency but people often made do quite adequately. Olive Sutton, one of the Guides at the camp in Rathfarnham, thought:

> The greatest hardship was having to eat brown bread and not having bananas. For a long time, a white loaf was better than cake, and bananas were a special treat. Clothing had been rationed as well as some food items such as tea and

sugar. We learned to sew, and mend our socks and stockings, and make do with many things for as long as they would last.

Paul Rowan, employed by his father in a seed-merchant company, recalled, 'We had plenty of butter, plenty of bread, plenty of everything. Members of the British Army [stationed in Northern Ireland] loved to come to Dublin for a treat, to Jammet's' – the gourmet French restaurant in Nassau Street.

Petrol rationing also meant that only doctors, army personnel and certain members of the government were allowed to use cars – unless you could get some fuel on the black market. Paul Rowan owned a black Ford Prefect and payed £2 a gallon – 'an enormous amount at the time because the going rate was 3s 6d' – to keep his car on the road. 'If you had a car everybody knew you.'

Lord Oranmore and Browne ran his old Ford V8 Woody Station Wagon on charcoal, made from the wood on the estate at Luggala. Most people, however, if they owned a car, had to keep it on blocks. In this way, Margaret Hamilton-Reid's Sunbeam Open Touring car's engine seized up, necessitating her purchase of the old Ford after the war.

The petrol shortage led to people taking to bicycles. Many thought nothing of cycling twenty-four miles from Roundwood to Dublin. The postman in Roundwood spent much of his time pedalling the five miles between Roundwood and Luggala. No sooner had he delivered one telegram than another would arrive, and off he would peddle again with a message for Lady Oranmore and Browne or Master Dominick Browne, the eldest son.

There was also a revival of horse-drawn traffic. A pony and trap was a common sight on country roads. There were buses but, as Olive Sutton remarked, they often didn't go where you wanted.

The St Kevin's Bus Company operated the only bus

service from Dublin to Roundwood and Glendalough. Following the original mail-coach route, it travelled along the old Long Hill Road, passing over a dangerously narrow bridge near Ballinastoe.

Road construction and maintenance were badly affected during this period by lack of supplies and shortage of funds. However, work continued on building roads to mountain bogs to improve access to turf. County Councils were given compulsory access to the boglands during the Emergency and this provided much seasonal employment for men such as Pat O'Brien from Roundwood. 'The Powerscourt Demesne and the Guinness Estate were both contracted for the purpose of procuring turf banks – almost everyone procured a piece of land on which to cut their turf,' wrote Pat O'Brien in an article in the *Roundwood Journal*. There might be four hundred men cutting turf out on the bogs near the Sally Gap on any one day. It was arduous work, cutting the turf into chunks with special shovels called *sláin*s and then stacking the chunks into elaborate piles to dry. In 1946 Pat O'Brien was working for Wicklow Council cutting turf for the mental hospital of Portrane. It was a bad year and most of the turf had no chance to dry out. 'You saw women trying to get a fire lighting, little children freezing with the cold. We'd get into bed at night and there'd be linen sheets on cold stone.'

Trains also ran on turf during the Emergency, when coal could not be imported from Britain. 'Trying to get steam out of turf wasn't easy. It could take all day to get from Heuston Station to Galway or Mayo in the west, and the train would have to stop in Athlone to reload with turf.'

The French girls had also heard that it rained a lot in Ireland, more than any other European country. What they did not know, though, was how bad that summer had turned out to be or that August 1946 would be the wettest for twenty years.

As their aircraft soared over Wales and the clouds began to thicken, Pat O'Brien on the bog, Pa Brennan poaching in the hills and the Wicklow County Council workers in the quarry were already wet through.

Eight

As the minutes became hours, the plane journey that they had looked forward to with such enthusiasm was beginning to seem interminable. The girls from Le Havre sang songs to pass the time. 'Like good little Guides, who must never be idle,' said Janine, 'we played, we sang – we always had to be active.' The other girls were chatting but not about the war.

The singing at the front of the cabin continued, led by Nicole, Antoinette Emo and Odile Lecoquière:

> *Quoi qu'il m'arrive*
> *J'ai toujours le sourire*
> *Je prends la vie, les choses du bon coté.*
> *En me disant qu'il peut arriver pire*
> *Et ça suffit pour me mettre en gaité.*

> [Whatever should happen to me
> I will keep smiling
> And look on the bright side of life.
> I only need to tell myself that worse things could happen
> And that's enough to lift my spirits.]

The girls were feeling the discomfort of being cooped up in a small space for too long, shifting positions, stretching their legs, trying to keep warm and yawning from lack of sleep. The comfort that we take for granted nowadays, even on cramped 'no frills' airlines, was completely absent on this flight of more than four hours. Lilette preferred to stand, holding the metal bar that ran along the side of the cabin, shifting her weight from one foot to another.

'But I was very timid,' said Janine. 'I was at the back — alone.'

Lilette, Chantal and Andrée were talking to some of the shyer girls, Ginette and Janine, in an effort to reassure and distract them. They were also chatting to the youngest one, *la Benjamine*, little Sylvia, who exuded a confidence that belied her age and size. Or rather they were shouting: the constant whirr of the engines blocked out almost every other sound and their shouts had to be accompanied by significant gestures.

Jacqueline Conort's borrowed shoes were pinching her feet. She asked Chantal if she could remove them for the journey. 'As long as you change back before we arrive in Dublin,' her Cheftaine replied. The girls must look impeccable when they got off the plane. Jacqueline changed into sandals with American rubber soles.

As *Tante Ju* droned on, the singing subsided and monotony set in. Although they were travelling at one hundred and twenty miles an hour, it felt like twelve. Françoise sat cross-legged on the floor and rested her head on the fire extinguisher. Using her beret as a pillow, she closed her eyes. At the front of the cabin, where Geneviève's face was growing paler, Nicole and Micheline tried to get some sleep. Antoinette Nattier's eyelids drooped as she fell into a fitful doze.

Although tired, the Cheftaines, Chantal, Lilette and Andrée, kept wide awake.

Some of the girls were beginning to feel pangs of hunger: the last food they had eaten was at six o'clock that morning.

As the clouds gathered beneath them and the plane began to vibrate increasingly through the air, the air hostess, Antoinette de Brimont, assured the Cheftaines that the juddering was quite normal. Having never flown before, they could make no comparisons.

'We were confident and naïve,' said Janine.

If they were suffering from a little queasiness, it was only to be expected and nothing to be alarmed about. Producing little lumps of sugar dipped in crème de menthe, the air hostess passed them around the cabin. Geneviève took a lump to quell the rising nausea in her stomach.

There was no seatbelt alarm – indeed, for the passengers, there were no seatbelts.

'At no time did the crew appear to be worried,' said Andrée Bonnet.

Antoinette Emo remembered the parting words of her parents in Le Havre: 'Make sure you send us a telegram when you get to Dublin saying *"Bien arrivée."*'

In the control tower at Dublin Airport, the officer on duty became aware of the French military plane for the first time when he received a message from the aircraft at 11.35 GMT, stating that it was *en route* from Le Bourget with an estimated arrival time of 12.15 GMT. It identified itself by the call sign 177B.

In 1946, Dublin Airport was a tiny place. 'You could walk your puppy round it,' said Margaret Hamilton-Reid. The Dublin terminal had been transferred from the military airfield at Baldonnel, County Dublin, to the newly constructed airport at Collinstown – twelve miles north of Dublin city centre – in 1940, when Aer Lingus ran its first commercial flight.

During the war years only a few thousand passengers used

the airport. At the end of 1945 this number had risen to twenty thousand. The sometimes-frenetic bustle that we associate with air travel today – queues snaking around foyers at check-in desks, boards flashing and constant tannoy announcements – was unheard of in those days. Passengers boarding flights to Croydon, Liverpool or Paris were advised to turn up only fifteen minutes before they were due to fly. Aer Lingus, which had come into being ten years earlier, was advertising eight flights a day in 1946. A return to Paris cost £23 8s 0d. When a white-collar worker could expect to earn about £300 a year, this represented almost one month's salary.

At Rineanna (Shannon Airport) one of the busiest days ever was recorded in *The Irish Times* on 19 August 1946: 'At least one plane arrived every hour between 9 A.M. and 5 P.M. ... the overworked staff were relieved to get an evening "breather".' At the beginning of the twenty-first century, in excess of seventeen million people pass through Dublin Airport each year. The skies hum with aircraft landing every few minutes. In 1946 commercial aviation was in its infancy. The first Aer Lingus flight to Europe had only touched down at Le Bourget in June of that year, heralding a new era of travel. The French Girl Guides were, therefore, some of the first air passengers from their country.

The technical sophistication of aviation that is taken for granted nowadays did not exist in 1946. There were no satellites, no global positioning system keeping the plane on track and no weather radars. Capitaine Habez only had minimal navigational equipment: his gyro compass, a radio-telegraphy transmitter and receiver, a weather forecast from Le Bourget of doubtful reliability and his wits. If he hit stormy weather, it wasn't going to be easy.

At 11.45 GMT, now tuned into the Dublin frequency of 405 kilohertz, the wireless operator informed Dublin that

177B was flying in cloud and descending. He also indicated that his radio was suffering some interference. Four minutes later, Adjutant Duran requested a bearing that would enable the plane to steer a course towards Dublin. They had flown over Cardiff and were leaving the coast of Wales.

Up to this point the crew was using what was known as the Gee system to navigate. Gee was a radio navigation aid that had been developed by Britain during the Second World War, primarily to assist their bomber offensive, and was first used exactly five years before, on 12 August 1941. Its usefulness over Germany varied with changes in the types of enemy jamming but it served continuously as an invaluable homing system for the Allies and was heavily relied upon during the D-Day landings.

The Gee system provided the navigator, Michel Tourret, with what was known as a 'fix' from pulses transmitted by three ground stations. The pulses were displayed on a cathode-ray tube on a screen in the cockpit and this enabled the navigator to accurately fix his position on a chart. As he continuously plotted his route from these intersecting signals, Aspirant Tourret's charts were a riot of criss-crossing lines.

The system operated in the VHF band and was hence altitude dependent: the higher the aircraft was in the sky, the more accurate the range. *Tante Ju* 177B was descending rapidly through cloud as it passed over Wales and the last fix the navigator received positioned the plane three miles south of its track. In 1946, the British Gee chains, including a temporary north-western chain that had a station in Northern Ireland, did not provide acceptable cover over the approaches to Dublin. (The Taoiseach, Eamon de Valera, was asked in 1944 whether he would allow a Gee chain to be built to cover mainly the west coast of Ireland but he turned down the offer.) An expert noted that 'no sensible navigator would ever have tried using the Gee chains for landing purposes in

Dublin'. As the plane left the Welsh coast to cross the Irish Sea, it was also leaving the coverage of the Gee system. With his visibility becoming significantly poorer, the pilot was now flying by reference to his on-board instruments alone.

As the weather continued to wreak havoc in the country and in the skies, the duty officer in the Dublin control tower was communicating with planes in the area every few seconds. The 12.03 from Liverpool wanted clearance for landing. The 12.06 departing for Croydon was ready to take off; and the plane due in at 13.06 from Croydon was looking for bearings from an altitude of 5,500 feet.

Still confident that he was on the right track, Capitaine Habez, although he could hear signals from the other aircraft, did not feel it was necessary to interrupt the overworked air-traffic controllers. Between pilots and navigators, an etiquette existed: a queuing system whereby it was courtesy to wait your turn. As the plane continued to shake on its downward path, he spoke over the intercom to the girls in the cabin: 'Ladies, in twenty minutes you will be sitting down at table with your Irish friends.'

At the time that the wireless operator requested a bearing, Dublin control asked the French plane to give its height. Adjutant Duran replied '400 metres' – that was only 1,300 feet.

The pilot requested a local weather report for Dublin. Throughout the flight he had depended on his forecast from Le Bourget but the weather was rapidly deteriorating as they crossed the sea. He received a report indicating that the surface wind was gusting to forty miles per hour and visibility was approximately three miles. The wind was clearly much stronger than that indicated from Le Bourget. Capitaine Habez started to climb out of the cloud, which was down to 300 feet, and adjusted his compass course to 340 degrees to counteract the effect of the strong winds that were driving his plane down, causing it to drift towards the coast.

At 12.08 Capitaine Habez revised his arrival time to 12.50.

At 12.18, when asked to give his height, he replied 680 metres – 2,000 feet above sea level.

A revised magnetic bearing was given to the pilot. This should have informed him that there had been a considerable change in the direction of the wind – a complete reversal, in fact. It was now blowing north-westerly. He was flying his plane into the eye of the storm: a deep depression that the meteorology station in Le Bourget had told him would no longer be in the area. If he did not adjust his compass course accordingly and divert his machine he was going to be in serious trouble.

But nothing more was heard that day from Capitaine Habez and his crew and nobody in Dublin Airport could say whether he had received the revised bearing or not.

Nine

An hour and a half after Eileen Beatty and Margaret Hamilton-Reid arrived at the airport, at 12.30 GMT, a clerical officer was sent up to the balcony of the control tower to listen out for the sound of motors in the sky. The officer was still listening an hour later.

The sound of engines *was* heard, but not from the balcony of the control tower at Collinstown.

A young boy, Larry Martin, walking along the beach near Courtown, County Wexford, heard a sound: a distant hum. The hum grew louder. Turning his face upwards in curiosity, the boy was just in time to see a plane appear out of the mist, very low in the sky. It seemed to take a right-hand turn along the coast towards Arklow.

Further up the coast, Arthur Tomkins was sitting in his hut with the door wide open, looking out over a 'miserable sea' at the northern end of Brittas Bay where the rocks jut out at Jack's Hole, more generally known as Ballinacarrig.

He recalled:

> It was about mid-morning when I suddenly heard the sound of an aeroplane approaching from the south, close to the

coast, but just out over the sea. Quickly looking out, I was able to catch a glimpse of the ghost of a plane as it passed, flying towards the north. I judged that it was not more than about 600 feet above the waves and not far beyond the end of the projecting line of rocks.

He watched the plane, barely visible in the mist and rain and 'obviously looking for landmarks', fly up and down the coast for ten or fifteen minutes.

If I had been near a telephone I would have attempted to communicate with Collinstown Airport. As the sound of the engines died away, I could tell that it had turned inland. I said to my wife, 'Where could that plane have come from? This is not a regular flight route. That pilot must have got lost and be following the coast, but he is very low. If he does not rise he will hit the Sugarloaf.

Still further north, on Dr Collis's farm near Newtown Mount Kennedy, Leo Ryan, a farm labourer, was working in an outhouse loft.

I was alone at the time and I heard a droning of a plane in the distance … it came right over the loft I was in. I looked out and it was just barely over the trees. It was so low that I stooped my head, as I thought it would strike me. It was going very slowly and only about twenty feet over the ground. It was making a terrible noise and was flying so near the house it had to rise to escape the trees. It then circled over a bog near the house. I kept watching and it then flew away … When I saw the plane at first it was coming out of heavy fog and I had a view of it again for about ten minutes. I thought at first that it was going to land. It was about 1.15 P.M. [12.15 GMT] at the time, as I was going to my dinner.

Half-way up the valley between Lough Tay and Lough Dan, close to the shooting lodge of Luggala, Hilary Hamilton was disturbed by a terrible roar of engines coming low over the two-storey house in Ballinrush where she was staying, on the banks of the Cloghoge River (about a thousand feet above sea level and about two hundred feet off the floor of the valley). 'You could hardly see the road about twenty feet away,' she reminisced recently to her son Richard, then just one year old. Although she didn't see it, she could hear the revving of the engines and she listened in amazement as a plane seemed to do a U-turn in the valley before heading north. The pilot, she decided, was obviously lost.

There were other tales: tales of people sitting round their turf fires, hearing the thunder of engines overhead. People talked of seeing a plane coming in very low over Kilcoole or Wicklow Head and then turning inland towards the mountains.

Ten

Mullaghcleevaun, Moanbane, Gravale, Kippure, Tonelagee, Table, Tonduff, War and Djouce, the broad granite domes that typify the landscape of Wicklow's harsh interior, are all over 2,000 feet high. To the south of these, Clohernagh, Carrawaystick, Croaghanmoira and Slievemaan, the high beds that circle the great Lugnaquilla, reach similar heights. Lugnaquilla, the highest of all the mountains in the Wicklow range, rises to 3,039 feet. The Sugarloaf is small in comparison, at just 1,654 feet.

Jolted from their half-slumber by the vibrations, a few of the girls let out gasps as *Tante Ju*, with its solid skin of corrugated alloy, lurched and dropped into a series of air pockets – *trous d'air*, a phrase that was not in the girls' vocabulary at the time. The plane was banking steeply to the left and the right. Feelings of incomprehension gave way to alarm as the plane continued to thud through the cloud.

As Daniel Duran carried on nimbly tapping out dots and dashes on his Morse key, the air hostess, Antoinette de

Brimont, was making her own dashes – in and out of the cabin. Putting on a brave face, she again distributed crème-de-menthe-soaked sugar lumps to the girls in an attempt to quell even her own mounting uneasiness. It was all she could do. No one was seriously worried, however. No one, not even the crew, had any idea how severe the storm was. The crew did not consider it necessary to put on their seatbelts.

Jacqueline was the first to notice the navigator through the little window panel. 'He was examining some chart, walking up and down and looking confused.'

If the navigator was confused, then so was the pilot. If his stomach muscles tightened and his heart began to beat uncomfortably fast, if beads of sweat appeared on his forehead, it was because, grappling with the contrary winds, his visibility was reduced to almost nothing. Grey, impenetrable clouds swept past his windscreen.

Nevertheless Capitaine Habez was confident of his bearings. He had steered his plane successfully over the Welsh coast and the crew could still hear other aircraft 'working Dublin' over the radio. At times he thought he glimpsed the sea through the dense clouds, although afterwards locals would speculate whether it was the large expanse of water of the Vartry Resevoir or one of the mountain lakes that he had caught sight of. Still wide-awake, Lilette, who had not slept at all during the flight, is convinced that what happened next was not a dream. 'We had a big fall. It was obviously a very significant drop. The pilot then spoke to us and said we had fallen several metres. I'm sure that this is what he told us.' The pilot would later deny that they had ever gone into a downdraught, as was reported in some newspapers. Lilette instinctively clung to the metal rail more tightly. She was standing in the middle of the plane.

As the plane bucked against another column of air, 'I went to sit in the toilet, as it was more comfortable,' said Jacqueline Conort. On the floor, Odile Lecoquière bent over, taking up a brace position to lessen the unpleasant effect the movement was having. She wasn't worried. 'I thought we were approaching the airport.'

Suddenly, a big black shape loomed in front of the pilot's eyes. It was a cigar-shape he was familiar with: the cloud formation that pilots call 'lent-cu'. He attempted to steer his plane underneath to obtain a better view.

A few seconds later, what he actually saw caused him, in a sickening spin of adrenaline, to pull back hard on the control column.

Capitaine Habez was the first to realise his terrible mistake, the first to notice that the plane with its crew of five and twenty-one passengers was on a collision course for a mountain. Ten seconds later, before the navigator had a chance to check his charts, it was too late.

'The plane appeared to fall,' recalled Janine, 'then nothing.'

Eleven

Pa Brennan, a strong twenty-one-year-old, had started poaching with his father when he was eight or nine years old. On 12 August, he set out alone in a blanket of mist at 6.30 A.M. Although he worked in his father's shop in Roundwood, he could often be found tramping the nearby hills during shop hours and this day was no exception. He had every intention of spending the whole day in the Wicklow Mountains. In the foul weather, it was hard dirty work – splashing through ferns, heather and long grass, slipping on slimy rocks, with the clouds obscuring the high mountains – but he loved it and he loved the landscape.

Unconcerned by the grey banks of cloud and the driving wind, he scrambled without falling, clutching the heather firmly and listening for the weird screech of the grouse on the wing. Like the wild clansmen before him, he knew every inch of the ground and he knew the meanings of all the old

Celtic place names too. 'You'd be there, waiting to poach deer, and you could see why the Celts had given the names they had to the rocks.' Tonelagee was the 'backside to the wind'; Lough Nahanigan, the 'lake of calamity'; Carrignashooke, the 'rock of the hawks'; and Luggala, the 'hollow of the hill' or 'hollow of sweet sounds'.

An earlier visitor to Ireland, the French Royalist Monsieur de la Tocnaye, had remarked on the eve of the 1798 rebellion: 'It is singular that there is not a single ancient name in this country which has not its special signification.'

Pa Brennan, like other villagers, always used local names to identify a stream or a sheep path in the area – names such as the Piper's Brook, Murdering Steps or the Barr. With an expert's eye for pheasant, woodpigeon, grouse or deer, he strode through the hills with his rifle slung over his thick shoulders. He was well known in the Associated Merchandise Company in Lower Oriel Street in Dublin, where he would sell his day's bounty. 'Four deer carcasses – very stale and smelly, £12 10s 0d,' read one of his receipts.

A mile from where Pa Brennan roamed, another Roundwood man, Pat O'Brien, and Sean Woodcock from Enniskerry were working for the Council near the Sally Gap. Though only eighteen miles from the General Post Office in Dublin's O'Connell Street, the Sally Gap was a lonely and desolate place and the clouds only intensified its sense of remoteness. Wild wastes of heather swelled and rolled away on every side of them.

The men were exposed to the full force of the weather and within minutes they were soaked. They suspected that a lot of the cut turf was already past saving: it stood in piles, sodden and useless.

Just like young men from the Enniskerry area such as Brian and Conor Hogan, Charlie Keegan or the doctor's son Bill Deely, the Roundwood locals Pat O'Brien and Pa Brennan knew the mountainous area intimately and they also knew its history. Beyond the hills, behind the shadows and along the distant ridges were the strongholds of Fiach MacHugh and the territories of the fighting O'Byrnes.

Down below, the glens echoed to the names of Michael Dwyer and Joseph Holt. Part of the Hogans' hotel, the Mount Maulin, was over four hundred years old. It had provided the last place of refuge for the 1798 rebellion leader Joseph Holt before he finally surrendered to Lord Powerscourt.

Pa Brennan regarded poaching as almost a patriotic act. 'That's one for old Ireland, one less for your man,' he intoned as the shots rang out over the Deerpark on Lord Powerscourt's estate. The locals could all recite Robert Emmet's speech from the dock – 'Let no man write my epitaph' – by heart.

Some time after noon, Sean Woodcock heard one loud clap of thunder: 'a terrible explosion. The weather was ferocious, with a scudding wind and lashing rain.' It died away as quickly and he wasn't sure where the noise came from, possibly Tonduff. He saw no lightning. He and the other Council workers took no more than a cursory glance towards where they heard the sound and continued blasting stone, stone that would be used to build the Glenmacnass Road to Glencree.

At the same time, Pa Brennan thought he heard a distant bang – it sounded like artillery fire but he couldn't say from where. He didn't hear any engines. He looked in the direction of the sound he heard from across the mountains. It resounded as the clouds moved in a solid mass along the great backbone of Wicklow. Much to Pa's chagrin, a startled deer scampered and a golden plover issued a mournful wheep.

Twelve

In total, 200 military aircraft are recorded to have crashed or force-landed in the twenty-six counties of Ireland during the war period, resulting in 223 fatalities among 800 airmen. However, because of strict censorship, news of an accident in one county or district was often not reported outside the area. British, US and German Luftwaffe planes came to grief over the country. Many planes coming from the US simply ran out of fuel. With limited radar, others slammed into mountains and exploded on impact. It was, therefore, not uncommon to see 'a lorry driving out of Baldonnel with bits and pieces of a crashed aircraft on board', noted Joseph Laffan. Even though it might not have been in the news at the time, 'it wasn't something you could miss'.

After the war, when censorship laws were relaxed, a military aircraft crashing on Irish soil was more newsworthy – especially if that aircraft was carrying civilians. It also prompted people to ask if it wasn't time to look at the safety of flight over Ireland, especially as air traffic seemed to be increasing on a daily basis. Planes were only machines, after all, and at the mercy of nature, which could come in the form of any ill wind. It was a hot topic of conversation and led to many letters in *The Irish Times*.

'Eventually of course, all air conveyances will be equipped with "eyes", which will enable the pilot to see clearly in all weather,' wrote Arthur Tomkins in a letter printed on 16 August 1946.

Another letter to the paper, on 19 August, read:

> As we are not accustomed yet to this wonderful mode of travel, the strapping to one's seat, studying instructions for the use of life preservers, may upset ladies and children when air pockets are travelled through at 250 miles per hour or a blanket of cloud mist blots out everything from sight. As a traveller who has been all over Europe, I would not hesitate to recommend this form of rapid and comfortable transport, as the element of real danger is almost infinitesimal and to people of normal sound nerves there is no need for anxiety when the plane is able to keep proper altitude.

'It is one thing to be quite safe and another to feel it,' wrote a passenger on 'the mid-day Aer Lingus machine to Dublin from Croydon' in a letter printed in *The Irish Times* on 17 August.

> I am sure that not one of my twenty fellow passengers in the machine — bad though the weather very obviously was — had the remotest idea that we could have been in any danger ... True, we had a few bumps on leaving Croydon, a few more spaced out during about ten minutes at some time in mid-journey, and some more during the last five to ten minutes while we skirted the green fields around Collinstown coming in. But during these periods which might have caused many first-time flyers, of which I would judge there to be many among the passengers, to feel anxious, the hostess stood facing rearwards, but near the front end of the cabin, smiling and chatting away to everyone within earshot, just as though she were holding a party of friends in the safety and solidity of her home. I am sure that the fact that there was practically no visibility and there was, I

believe, an unsteady gale of fifty miles an hour blowing, accompanied by torrential rain, all passed unnoticed. All of us eventually entered the airport, feeling that perhaps the journey might have been more pleasant, and grumbling a little that we had been unable to see the country and sea over which we had flown, that was the extent of our emotion.

On 12 August, as the passengers from Croydon brushed past them on their onward journeys, oblivious to anything untoward, Margaret Hamilton-Reid and Eileen Beatty paced the airport foyer. 'It was a time of great tension,' remembered Margaret Hamilton-Reid. 'A civilian flight from Paris had come in on time – it was announced by microphone – but *this* one wouldn't have been announced – it was a private plane.'

In the control office, all contact with 177B had been lost since 12.18 GMT, when a message had come through from the wireless operator that the plane was at a height of 680 metres. The airport staff had no idea where the plane was now. It could have landed in Wales or it could have turned back for France. If so, it probably had enough fuel. This was the best they could hope for.

Their worst fear was that it had plummeted into the Irish Sea.

At 13.45 GMT Dublin Airport dispatched the following message to Seaforth Radio:

> Ju-52 call sign 177B due DW from Le Bourget at 12.50 GMT. Unheard since 12.15 GMT. Last QTE 141 true at 11.59 GMT. Please advise shipping.

Two Avro Anson search planes were sent out to patrol the Dublin area and the Welsh coast. Lifeboats were put on stand by.

'I remember the authorities coming up to Eileen Beatty

and myself and saying there was no point in waiting any longer.' At three o'clock Margaret Hamilton-Reid and Eileen Beatty reluctantly left the airport. It wasn't easy. 'We left not knowing what had happened.' As they drove back to Rathgar, the sky was a dark slate grey and the gutters flowed. Eileen Beatty informed Mrs Lillis and The Irish Girl Guides in South Frederick Street of the events. She passed on the bad news to Moira Cooke in the Country Shop, where the sandwiches were already beginning to curl.

There was no further communication from *Tante Ju*. 'The general view was that it had gone down off the Kish Lighthouse,' said Miss Hamilton-Reid.

Thirteen

Before anybody had a chance to be frightened, one of the doors of the Junkers plane burst open, scooping in lumps of turf as pieces of the aircraft broke away.

Chantal de Vitry recalled a bone-jarring thud as if someone was striking the skin of the aircraft with a wrench. There was then a sickening sound: a grating crunch as if parts underneath were snapping away. Suddenly the floor collapsed beneath them.

Jacqueline's nose smashed against the toilet door, which failed to open. Nicole's glasses shot from her face. It was the last time Chantal saw the flagpole of the 75th Paris Company, which slipped from her grasp.

Françoise remembered a hurtling sensation. Life seemed to be going by like a film on fast-forward. Everything was in disarray. The plane then appeared to rebound in the air and strike the ground a second time, with even greater force. There was a sound of glass shattering, metal crunching. Earth and branches hurtled through the cabin at a horrible speed. Geneviève's legs fell through the hole created when sections of the metal floor at the front of the cabin, above the fixed landing gear, gave way on the first impact. On the second impact the floor panels were pushed back again, trapping her legs underneath, and a searing, astounding pain shot through her body. An equally terrible pain tore through Magali Noyer's scalp and Anne Lemonnier's ribs.

The pain ripped through the cabin, overwhelming the other Guides. Bones cracked and were pushed out of place: femurs, tibias, clavicles broke through the protective cover of human skin. Jaws and knee-joints were fractured. Flesh was lacerated and noses were dislocated. Blood seeped from cut skin onto pristine skirts, dresses and capes.

As they were thrown forwards and on top of each other, Guide and Eclaireuse became indistinguishable, a tangle of twisted limbs, a blur of navy blue and chestnut brown, mixed together in a jumble of concussion and contusions.

'Chaos took the place of order,' Quidnunc later reported in his 'Irishman's Diary' column.

> In a single second the plane … was disintegrating. The engines went, ripped from their seating. The massive tyres were flung on one side. The undercarriage collapsed. The root of the portside wing crumpled. Showers of mud and turf poured into the cabin. The once airborne machine was suddenly at rest, a crumpled lifeless thing.

There followed one long moment of silence.

As the stricken machine was hurtling through the sky, Lilette had continued to clutch on to the metal rail that ran along the side of the cabin. She later said that it acted as a sort of seatbelt.

Four years earlier Lilette Brune, as she was then called, had enrolled at the university in Toulouse as a student of mathematics. Travelling the fifteen kilometres to college every day, she had befriended another student on the train and quickly revealed her Jewish identity to her. 'You are a fool to tell me this,' her friend had told her. 'You don't know who I am.'

It soon transpired that her new friend and her mother were involved in the Resistance and knew all about the need for keeping silent. Lilette soon joined her friend's meetings. It was common for French of Jewish faith or origin to lead or become part of Maquis operations in the south and Lilette was soon helping to organise supply drops to assist other Maquis smuggling refugees across the Spanish border. She told her parents, in the event of her being caught by the Germans, it was better to have done something than nothing at all.

'I was eighteen and without fear – it was like a game.'

But this new game had suddenly become disorganised – *'tout le grand jeu a été désorganisé'*. As the memory of her student days careened into her head, Lilette braced herself for the impact.

As arms, legs and bodies were hurled against each other and against the walls of the cabin, Lilette kept her eyes shut and continued to grip the bar until *Tante Ju* eventually shuddered to a halt. She felt only a slight twinge in her left arm.

Knowing that the plane's engines were vulnerable, her first thought was to get the door open as quickly as possible and get clear of the machine. That same year, Lilette's uncle had narrowly escaped with his life after jumping from a plane that had crashed near Marseilles. The aircraft then burst into flames, killing the remaining passengers.

Turning to the other girls, however, and seeing the blood all over Agnès' face, Nicole's leg turned back on itself and Geneviève, who seemed to have almost disappeared through the floor, her second and overriding thought was that she seemed to be the only one to have escaped unscathed.

Much later, Lilette would make light of the fact that they couldn't have been very good Guides to have ended up on a plane that completely lost its way. As somebody later wrote to her, 'it really was embarrassing, to be a group of Guides in a plane and then to go the wrong way.

'There were people waiting for us at the aerodrome and we had hit a mountain ...'

Having lost consciousness for a moment, Andrée Bonnet woke, confronted by a 'spectacle of desolation' and the smell of engine oil. Like Lilette, she had the impression that she was the only one who could stand up. Her immediate impulse was also to get out of the plane.

With much hammering, considerable effort and a mounting sense of urgency, Andrée and Lilette tried to work the long lever of the cabin door. It was jammed but suddenly gave way, admitting the cold outside air, which hit their cheeks like a whip. Looking at the bleak scene before them, Lilette imagined they had landed on water. The rushes and grass, flattened and swaying in the wind and rain, looked like waves breaking on the sea.

However, for Andrée the sight of Capitaine Habez remained in her memory. 'I was astonished to see the pilot opening the door from the outside.' With his forehead bleeding from a blow from the steering wheel, he had crawled out of the plane through the cockpit door.

Then Chantal appeared, as if in a dream. She was also outside the plane, helping the pilot and looking around. She was taking in the horror of their situation and what to her was the miracle of their continued existence.

For Chantal and Andrée, shocked into action, the necessity to do something immediately became absolute. Standing exposed to the full force of the weather, the driving rain stung their faces. The wind was gusting fiercely and a grey mass of clouds blotted everything out of sight.

There were a few scattered tufts of grass and lumps of heather and moss but it was impossible to see in any direction. The fog, resting directly above them, made it feel as if winter had come early to this place. Clambering over the soft ground, it felt as if they had come down on a piece of waterlogged waste.

Signalling to Lilette that they were going to look for help, they assured her that they would not be long. In the meantime, Lilette, with the danger of fire dispelled from her mind, set about untangling 'an indescribable confusion of jumbled bodies and broken limbs inside the battered plane'.

Ignoring whatever pain they felt, Chantal, Andrée and Capitaine Habez set off together. They climbed higher up the slope of a hill, where the ground changed to lichen-covered rock and loose pieces of mica schist but little relieved the lunar landscape. Surveying the scene in all directions, they could see only a bleak, treeless region: the mist was so thick, the driving rain so cold, there was nothing to indicate they were on a mountain at all, let alone surrounded by other mountains.

Removing a compass from his pocket, Capitaine Habez took a reading and they struck off in a northerly direction, towards where he thought Dublin was, leaving the remnants of the plane and its occupants sitting on a dark-brown bog.

Fourteen

The Irish bog has fired the imagination of poets, writers and artists for generations and Ireland has some of the last intact bog in Europe. It is the most fundamental of landscapes, connecting right back with Ireland's pagan past. It is an ancient and fragile upland, with plants sitting on the corpses of their ancestors, going back as much as ten thousand years. Sometimes the bog reveals hidden treasures too: artefacts such as necklaces and swords and even remains of human beings, placed there in Celtic times, lying undisturbed for generations.

No one in the plane, however, was thinking about the bog's rich history. At that moment, for those conscious enough, it felt as if they had fallen onto another planet.

The force of the impact had thrown everyone forwards and on top of each other. It was impossible to know who was seriously injured or who was simply trapped under another body, unable to move. The left side of the plane was crushed and the worst injuries seemed to be sustained there.

Little by little, others regained consciousness and started to groan.

Lilette began by asking those who could walk to come to

the back of the plane. Three girls crawled to their feet – Antoinette Nattier, Eliane Lemonnier and Monique Ygouf: the three from Cherbourg.

Antoinette Nattier was one of the first to become aware of her surroundings. 'I opened my eyes – everybody was on the floor. On my right was a girl with an open fracture of the knee.' In a trance-like state, she managed to move by climbing over the bodies of other girls, ignoring their moans. Many years later, she was amazed that she had 'no memory of communicating with anybody'. Although shivering with the cold, from the rain and wind blowing through the open door of the half-crushed cabin, she used her cape to cover one of the more seriously injured girls.

Monique was also able to scramble to the tail of the plane. Her skirt and cape were torn. There was blood on her legs but she noted that it wasn't her own. Blood was trickling out of Antoinette Emo's ankle and the bone was exposed. Her arm trapped, and bleeding badly, Agnès Laporte lay on her side motionless.

The seats were twisted and on top of each other, trapping the rucksacks underneath. Eliane looked around her in dismay, 'It was terrible – many of the girls were seriously injured. They were groaning and we could do nothing.' The three uninjured girls, Antoinette Nattier, Monique and Eliane – *les trois valides*, as they were later called – set about assisting their Cheftaine, Lilette.

Janine was aware that Antoinette, Monique and Eliane had detached themselves from the pile of bodies in front of her and gone to the back of the plane. 'I don't know how many minutes elapsed. I "woke up" lying on a pile of bodies,' she said.

> I got up dazed and saw that the back door of the plane was open. I went through this door and found myself sinking into sodden, soft earth. I was once again on the edge of

fainting: dulled, inert and stupefied. Somebody leant over
me, picked me up and made me get back into the plane. I
sat down on the seat that I had occupied during the flight.
I wasn't in pain but I had the impression that my left arm
was detached from my body. I didn't move; I didn't speak –
to whom? I waited.

Concussed and confused, Françoise stared out of the
porthole. She saw that the engine under the left wing was
missing, the fuselage bashed. 'I said to myself, "Good, we will
be arriving with one engine missing."' She then saw that her
cape was spattered with blood, which was seeping on to her
dress. Somebody said to her, 'Françoise, I'm cold.' Françoise
Béchet enveloped a girl in her cape. She lapsed into uncon-
sciousness with her head resting on the fire extinguisher.

Gradually others started to regain consciousness. Later
some would recall fractured conversation: '"Do not move,"
then groans. I fell back into semi-consciousness,' remembered
Odile Lecoquière. 'Then I felt my leg burning. Was there a
fire? But I did not react. A great weight was suffocating me.'
She felt she had to get out.

'Don't touch!' screamed somebody.

Nicole woke to the sound of Sylvia. The little Jewish girl
from Gentilly had let out the biggest scream of all, 'There has
been a CRA-ASH! A CRA-ASH!' She had fallen through the
floor but was in less pain than those at the front of the plane,
who had taken the brunt of it. 'I was in this kind of hole. It
was dirty and I was so cold that I had little movement in my
leg. I remember pushing a girl whose leg was broken and she
shrieked in pain.'

'I lost my memory for a long time – on the ground, not
being able to move,' said Catherine de Geuser. When she
awoke she didn't know the answers to any questions that
concerned her. 'I no longer knew who I was or where I was. It
was very dark and I was cold.' Her eyes could not make sense
of anything. 'I didn't even know that I was lying in a plane.'

Antoinette Emo had also lost any sense of where she was. She was incredulous when told they had been in a plane crash. What was she doing there? How had she escaped?

Her knee completely turned around, Anne Lemonnier was unconscious under twisted metal.

Surrounded by pieces of earth, the air hostess, Antoinette de Brimont, lay on the floor unable to speak or move, crème-de-menthe sugars littered about her feet.

Inside the toilet, Jacqueline Conort from Le Havre drifted in and out of consciousness, dark rings already beginning to form round her eyes. Her borrowed shoes had been thrown across the cabin. In the toilet, she was still wearing sandals with American rubber soles.

The Guide Law

A Guide's honour is to be trusted
A Guide is loyal
A Guide's duty is to be useful and to help others
A Guide is a friend to all and a sister to every other
Guide
A Guide is courteous
A Guide is a friend to animals
A Guide obeys orders
A Guide smiles and sings under all difficulties
A Guide is thrifty
A Guide is pure in thought, word and deed

UK Guiding, 1946

Fifteen

'Do you know the thing most troublesome to find in this soft, wet, dewy, pelting summer? It is water. It's never where you want it.'

Seán O'Faoláin, *Sunday Independent*, 1946

The light was beginning to fade. The two Cheftaines, Chantal and Andrée, and the captain had been gone for hours. The door of the plane was half-hanging off its hinges. The wind blew through the opening, as the storm fretted above and around the plane. Rain was dripping through the cracks in the roof. The girls were huddled together in the fuselage, marooned in this cave-like structure that had become their only refuge, perched over an inhospitable bog in thick swirling cloud. Even though it was August, it was icily cold – the cold penetrated their bones and their senses. They were tired and hungry and, ironically, despite the continuously dripping water, they were extremely thirsty.

Cut and bleeding, it was Nicole Jacques-Léon who started the singing again:

Quoi qu'il m'arrive
J'ai toujours le sourire . . .

A Guide smiles and sings under all difficulties. In 1946, this was the eighth Guide Law.

In founding the Scout and Guide movements, Lord Baden-Powell and his wife had set out to provide training designed to not only give pleasure but also help in the development of character. It aimed to promote physical and moral health. Children learnt about honour and duty as well as how to tie knots and hoist a flag. Girls were taught practical skills, even survival skills such as B.P. had learned during the Boer War.

Singing round the campfire, sleeping under canvas, dancing and recounting stories, these were activities that all the Guides and the Eclaireuses had embraced with a passion after the constraints of the war.

When many companies had been forced to go underground during the occupation, meeting clandestinely in private houses or churches – Chantal's 75th Paris Company had continued to meet in the tower of the church of St Pierre de Chaillot – and others had ceased meeting altogether, Scouting and Guiding had started up with renewed vigour after peace was declared.

'It was very important for us to put on our uniforms again,' recalled Janine. In her ruined town of Saint Lô, 'where everything needed to be rebuilt, solidarity expressed itself in all sorts of ways'. People were anxious to move forward, to put the bad years behind them and reinforce peace again.

The Guides de France and Eclaireuses had come through the war. They had survived. They were on the threshold of life.

And so they sang. Antoinette Emo, Janine and *les trois valides*, Eliane, Monique and Antoinette Nattier, joined in with Nicole.

Sing at danger, smile under pain!

There were moments of macabre humour. 'I looked down at Nicole's leg', said Antoinette Emo, 'and shrieked, "Good heavens. Have you seen your tibia?"' It was sticking out of the skin with a big open gash. Later she remarked how 'that had soon shut up her singing'.

Micheline, unable to move herself, looked on helplessly as cold water from the roof of the plane intermittently dripped into the hole in Nicole's knee. When she looked out through a porthole, Micheline saw what she thought was long grass waving.

Geneviève, her legs turned back on each other, was staring out of the hole she had fallen into after the floor collapsed, gritting her teeth. Attempting to lighten the mood, Lilette said to her, 'What are you doing down *there*? I didn't realise we had a dwarf on board.'

Looking into Lilette's eyes, Geneviève saw a glint of amusement but she also detected an underlying concern. Geneviève began 'thinking of those that I had left behind. Having lost my younger brother in a car accident in 1939, I was saying to myself, it would be too much for my parents if I were to die as well.' Geneviève's eyes closed, then opened. She wanted to cry out but she tensed herself and smiled.

Between the singing and the crying, some of the girls were thanking God out loud that nobody was dead and they prayed: 'God will protect us.' Save us, save us, they seemed to say. Let God, in his infinite mercy, not abandon us, in darkness and in pain.

'That's ridiculous,' retorted Sylvia sharply, 'because if your God existed, we would not have had this crash!'

Faith and scepticism vied with each other but the best hope they had now was solidarity, trying to keep as warm as possible from arm on arm.

Lilette kept on working. She did not mention her own background. 'I didn't know that Lilette was a Jew,' said Sylvia later, 'or that she didn't believe in God either. We didn't speak about such things.'

Occasionally there were moments of silence, each girl in total solitude. The silence was punctuated by moans, less frequent bursts of song and the sound of the wind and pelting rain outside. And in the mass of emotions, above all, there was no panic. 'No panic at all,' said Lilette.

Resigned one moment, impatient the next, Eliane Lemonnier suddenly heard a bleating outside. She looked out of the cabin and, squinting through the fog, spotted a sheep. With Monique, she ventured out of the broken machine to 'follow the beast, hoping that it might have strayed from a shepherd or shepherd's hut'. The sheep disappeared into the fog almost as soon as it appeared. 'We came to an iron stake, bent and broken.' For an instant they thought they smelled the odour of the sea but it was overpowered by a more rancid smell: bog water and engine oil.

Tripping over a few bits of debris, stones and muck, they gave up and retraced their steps to the plane. Defeated and powerless, there was nothing to do but wait.

Sixteen

At the foot of the mountain from which it took its name, the Mount Maulin Hotel, concealed from the road and set in a picturesque wooded spot, was a popular stopping-off point for walkers and locals alike. It commanded a fine view of the Sugarloaf to the south-east and the Scalp beyond Enniskerry. Known locally as the Silver Fox Farm, it had long since ceased breeding beavers and foxes. Its owners, Mr and Mrs Patrick Hogan, had bought the hotel as a going concern in the twenties.

A native Irish speaker, Patrick Hogan was a convivial man. Friends and neighbours would often pop by to converse on a wide range of subjects, from politics to the origin and meaning of local place names: Bahana, the townland in which they lived, meant the 'place of birch trees'; Enniskerry was the 'ford of the rocky ledge'; and the Great Sugarloaf was really Slieve Cualainn.

Much as he liked to talk, Mr Hogan did not usually greet the driver of the Johnston, Mooney and O'Brien bread van when it crunched up the drive every morning. His practical wife, Catherine, looked after the affairs of the hotel, a job she undertook with quiet efficiency. She was responsible for keeping the ten bedrooms spick and span and putting the food on the table. She employed two members of staff: Molly Coogan cooked and Madge Carroll acted as maid and waitress.

The hotel had a pleasant alpine feel to it, Bill Deely recalled, with its welcoming log fire and little dispensing bar. George Davis, an elderly artist who lived with his wife in a little house in the Deerpark a mile away, would regularly pop by for a hot toddy and a chat. The conversations often went on well into the night. Mr Davis usually took a short cut across a field from the Deerpark, climbing over a fence into the Hogans' land, which marked the boundary of the Powerscourt Estate.

The hotel had the reputation of being something of an Irish 'salon' and attracted other artists too. Camille Souter, the painter, was a regular caller.

After the Second World War, the house, which had once sheltered Joseph Holt, once again became a place of refuge. A few Austrian, German and Polish refugees settled in the Glencree valley and the Hogans welcomed these visitors into their lounge. Some of them remained in Ireland. One of the Hogans' sons, Conor, later married Analise Fuchs, the daughter of an Austrian refugee, whose family had settled in Bray. On 12 August 1946, a regular guest from Austria, Fraulein Frances Widman, was staying at the hotel.

The cosmopolitan nature of the clientele rubbed off on the Hogans' other son, Brian, who later took a great interest in languages and travel.

When a young woman in a 'pitiable condition' appeared at the hotel, it was Brian and Fraulein Widman who opened the door.

Continuing their journey across a wilderness of uneven heather and rushes, Chantal, Andrée and Capitaine Habez were constantly presented with fresh challenges. As one foot sank into the cold slime of a bog hole, another struck against a hidden rock. Marsh, gorse, stones, driving rain and wind hampered their crossing.

One of the many pieces of advice in Lord Baden-Powell's book *Scouting for Boys* was: if you are going to a new place, you should always look round every so often to take in the scene from the opposite direction so that you will more easily find your way back. After more than two hours of wandering, Chantal, Andrée and the pilot seemed to be going in circles. When they looked back, even though their eyes had become more accustomed to the gloom, the visibility was no more than about three yards. All they could see was grey fog.

Eventually, sinking into squelchy ground covered by sedge, they reached some rusty metal fencing and a wall. Capitaine Habez consulted his compass again.

Descending into a valley, the vegetation changed and they were soon swamped by a liberal supply of fern, its fronds the dark-green colour of summer. They cut their hands when they tried to use it for support. Mud-spattered and grazed, they lurched forwards.

They came to a thin trickle of brown bog water, glistening under wet moss, with one or two scattered tufts of rushes sticking out. As they followed the trickle, it widened into a stream. They stumbled downwards with the stream on their right-hand side. The stream turned into a river, accelerating with its onward rush, and eventually joined another wider river in spate.

The pilot was ready to leap. 'No!' Chantal and Andrée cried together. 'We cannot do it.' They struggled up to a narrower point of the river.

The pilot jumped first. He held out his hand for Chantal. A sharp pain stabbed her side as she drew in her breath. She jumped and fell gasping onto the bank on the other side. Now it was Andrée's turn. She was hesitant. Her foot was hurting and her energy reserves were flagging. As she faltered, her good foot struck empty air and her hands clawed uselessly at the slippery, muddy bank. Her two companions looked on as she tumbled waist deep into the brown, swollen waters. They could do nothing.

Water streamed into her mouth. She felt her skirt being pulled down. My last hour has arrived, she thought, and she heard herself screaming as the icy coldness of the river pressed on her skin. And as she felt herself falling an emotion suddenly swept through her: she was dreaming of her mother, her little town of Issoire, the Thursday meetings of the Guides de France and the Sunday outings she always looked forward to.

Her reverie was abruptly interrupted when she felt her body being slammed against something solid. Her nails were splintered as she grasped at a rock jutting out of the water. She coughed, spluttered and took in a mouthful of air.

The rock, however, checked Andrée's flow. She righted herself and next, with a strength that came from who knows where, managed to clutch the bank where Chantal and the pilot reached out to her and hauled her out of the water. She lay panting on the ground, her skirt torn and rucked up almost around her waist, her face deathly pale.

Weak-kneed, she thought she could not go on. But getting to her feet, she did. They all walked on, then stopped, walked again, then stopped, Andrée limping.

Slowly the three made their way downwards, following the widening river. The pilot was breathing hard, sweat on his face, his own hidden reserves ebbing away. As they descended further into the valley, the mist began to lift. A few scattered trees protected them from the wind. Pausing for a moment, they surveyed their surroundings. They were on top of a cliff.

Hundreds of feet below on the grassy floor, where the air was still, Chantal could discern blue smoke. It was rising vertically from the turf fire of a little cottage in the deep valley below. They could still hear the wind blowing through the trees but they did not hear the steady, reverberating noise of water. They did not know that they had arrived at the end of a valley above Ireland's highest waterfall.

Seventeen

In the grounds of St Columba's College in Rathfarnham, oblivious to the unfolding drama in the mountains ten miles away, the Irish Girl Guides were pitching their tents.

Olive Sutton arrived from Sligo with her sister Vera. They were looking forward to meeting the French and Dutch Guides and to the prospect of the camp, the first since the war in Europe. 'When we got to the camp, we found that there were Guides there from all parts of Ireland,' Olive Sutton recalled, 'although a large number were from Dublin.' The Irish Girl Guides were allocated the field at the side of the school building. Their tents were bell-shaped and they were to sleep six to a tent, feet to the pole in the middle. Captains would sleep in small single bivouacs.

The camp medical officer was Dr Johnson and Olive Sutton remembered her being a 'very large woman sleeping in a very small tent'. In charge of the camp was Estelle Moore from Cork, who spoke excellent French.

While the Irish Girl Guides settled in, awaiting the arrival of the French contingent, they played games. Despite the atrocious weather, they foraged about the grounds collecting leaves and branches that could be used to make tables and chairs or to build a campfire. Always active, they sat around in circles with their Patrol Leaders singing songs and telling stories.

A Patrol Leader herself, Olive Sutton wore two white stripes on the breast pocket of her shirt and the badge of her patrol, which was a kingfisher. Under the Patrol Leaders were the Seconds, who wore one white stripe. The girls had badges sewn on to their sleeves showing that they had passed exams in useful things such as first aid, child nursing, cooking, signalling, needlework or knitting. Olive and the other Guides compared badges. They each wore a specially folded tie over their uniforms, which could double up as a sling if anyone was hurt.

Margaret Hamilton-Reid was now back with her aunt in Rathgar, the old Ford parked in the drive, the flowers in the garden looking fresh as the rain continued to pelt against the patio windows. It was only a matter of time before the Guides at the camp in Rathfarnham were told of the calamity. She reflected on how exciting those summer camps were for everyone involved and how their spirits would be dampened by the news.

Things had changed since she had first joined the Guides in the early twenties. In those days, it had been entirely Protestant and very pro-British. 'I didn't question that I was promising loyalty to the king.' She was only fourteen then and thought 'nothing of carrying the Union Jack in Rathfarnham Parish Church'.

The seeds of change, however, had been sown. Her mother, although from a Presbyterian family in Monaghan and steeped in Unionism, was very conscious that the Catholics were being treated as second-class citizens and it 'made her very radical'. When a procession of Irish soldiers passed by their home one day, wearing their green uniform, Margaret Hamilton-Reid remembered her mother saying, '"See those soldiers over there? Those are our soldiers: they're Irish soldiers." It was the first time I ever saw the green uniform in my life.'

As anti-British feeling grew during the Troubles of the 1920s, the Guides were told to keep their hats – 'those big, stiff-brimmed hats' – in the parish hall so that they wouldn't be seen. 'It wasn't quite safe to walk with them on.'

Even though The Irish Girl Guides was still very much a Protestant preserve – names such as Findlater, Figgis, Guinness and Hyde predominated – the organisation had always been open to all creeds. Mrs Lillis, Area Commissioner for Dublin, was a Catholic and Catholic companies, such as the Dun Laoghaire Sea Rangers, were beginning to spring up all over the country. The Catholic Girl Guides of Ireland had been established since 1933. As she watched the rain dripping off the leaves and flowers in her garden, Margaret Hamilton-Reid imagined the Guides at the camp, in their much more practical uniform, getting ready, full of enthusiasm to greet their foreign guests.

Sometime in the evening, before they ate the supper prepared by their Quartermaster, Miss Findlater, the Irish Girl Guides were told that the French Guides would not be joining them.

Eighteen

'The reader is earnestly cautioned against any attempt to scale the steep face of the mountain ... adjacent to the waterfall. Roped together, and provided with suitable equipment, experienced rock-climbers could do it with no more than normal risk. For the ordinary man in everyday clothes to attempt it is a form of madness born of ignorance, that has led to more than one young life being cruelly dashed out at the boulder-strewn foot of this precipice.'

The Guide to Bray and Environs

George Davis and Brian Hogan had helped many an unfortunate person who had got into trouble where the 390-foot great white streak of foam crashed spectacularly down into the Deerpark before running through a glen to the sea. The area above the waterfall, known as the Glensoulan Valley, formed part of the ancient territory of Fercullen. A secluded spot, in 1946 it was one that few people penetrated.

Chantal, Andreé and Capitaine Habez could see the smoke from the cottage tantalisingly near at the bottom of an almost vertical cliff face. What drove them forward was a kind of rashness and inexplicable strength, which Chantal believed was possibly divine.

Immune to their cuts and scratches, they clasped at rocks, branches and earth as they crawled down the sheer drop – everything seemed to come away in their hands. Stones were only waiting to hurtle into the valley below on the slightest pressure. Clinging to each other to stop themselves slipping, they sometimes had to sit down and glissade in the mud.

'How they succeeded in getting down the cliffs at the side of the waterfall was a mystery we could never understand,' said Brian Hogan. 'It was a wonderful feat of courage and endurance.'

When they slumped to the ground at the bottom, a sign announced: 'DANGER OF ROCKFALLS. CLIMBING STRICTLY FORBIDDEN.'

Half an hour later Andrée and Capitaine Habez were sitting by the fire in the Davis's cottage in the Deerpark but Chantal's journey was not over yet.

As the three survivors dragged themselves towards the little house, the pilot was stumbling. His forehead was smeared with blood. He looked as if he might not make it to the door.

Engrossed in their own thoughts, few words passed between them towards the end of their ordeal. Despite her fatigue, Andrée, covered in mud and her uniform in tatters, was practising sentences in English in her head. Her main preoccupation was how to explain 'where the plane was as quickly as possible'. When the old couple opened the door of their cottage, Andrée was amazed to discover that the pilot spoke excellent English, so she let him do the talking.

Having spent several years in England during the war, Capitaine Habez was fluent in English. He told the astonished George Davis that he was the pilot of a plane and that his aircraft, with several passengers on board, had crashed somewhere near a big waterfall in a 'north-west direction', according to his compass. He explained that the three survivors had struggled down a mountain until they came to a fence and a river. He was too exhausted to speak any more.

Andrée and the captain collapsed inside the Davis's cottage, unable to move. Andrée recalled being put to bed with 'a nice cup of tea'.

But the nearest phone was over a mile away.

'Hurry up, hurry up,' urged George Davis to Chantal as he led her through a field, taking the short-cut route from the Deerpark towards Bahana. The pain in her ribs was excruciating; it sometimes took her breath away but, in a way, she was grateful for it. It helped her to concentrate and distracted her from the reality of what had happened on the mountain. She took one step, then another – each felt as if it might be her last – and finally arrived at the Mount Maulin Hotel. Having safely deposited her at the hotel, the elderly George Davis returned to his cottage in the Deerpark.

According to Brian Hogan, Chantal 'was a fine-looking girl of about twenty years wearing only a thin torn dress, soaked to the skin, covered in mud, cut and scraped on her face, hands and legs from falling down among the rocks and briars'.

Fraulein Widman opened the door and Chantal de Vitry, the twenty-one-year-old Cheftaine from the 75th Paris Company who two days earlier had been on holiday with her family near the Luberon hills, told her story to the Austrian guest who spoke fluent French.

Nineteen

At 6.45 P.M. an orderly at Bray Garda Station took an urgent phone call from Sergeant Wickham in Enniskerry, informing him that a plane had crashed. In 1946 communication by telephone happened in a roundabout way, as messages were relayed from exchange to exchange. The orderly immediately passed on the news to his superior, Superintendent Quinn.

Sergeant Wickham also rang the senior control officer, Patrick Murphy, in Dublin Airport, who told his principal, Mr O'Driscoll.

Leo Wickham, a former boilermaker, reported his story in a matter-of-fact way. The forty-six-year-old sergeant confirmed that

> a Mr Hogan had conveyed the message to the Enniskerry station. Mr Hogan, the proprietor of the Mount Maulin Hotel, was only able to say that a young lady had arrived at his door, exhausted and badly shocked, stating that she was one of a party of ladies on board a plane bound from Le Bourget Airport in Paris to Dublin. She had told him that the plane had crashed into the mountains and that the passengers and crew were injured, how badly she did not know. She had left to get assistance. The lady could give no idea where the plane was located beyond that she had

walked for about five hours over the mist-bound mountains
in heavy rain until she came to a fence and a river.

Sergeant Wickham then sent one of his officers to Prosser's
Bar, just down the road from the station, to seek out some
local advice.

Patrick Murphy, the control officer at Dublin Airport,
immediately called off the Anson and lifeboat search of the
sea. He also rang Dublin fire station. In the meantime,
Superintendent Quinn informed the garda headquarters in
Dublin and all the surrounding garda stations, whose men
were drafted in to help trace the location of the plane. They
rang all available first-aid organisations: local doctors, the
Irish Red Cross, St John Ambulance, local ambulances and
Dun Laoghaire fire station. The control officer put a call
through to the military authorities at Portobello Barracks in
Dublin and St Bricin's military hospital on Infirmary Road
on the north side of Dublin. The orderly officer in charge of
St Bricin's stated that he would do 'everything he could to
meet the situation'. Three military ambulances and three
army doctors were immediately dispatched to the Enniskerry
area and the hospital was told to prepare itself to accept any
casualties. St Michael's Hospital in Dun Laoghaire was put
on full alert.

Patrick Murphy phoned Monsieur Rivière in the French
Legation and the Secretary of The Irish Girl Guides, Eileen
Beatty. Finally he put through a call to the control officer at
Shannon Airport.

Abandoning their packing and any thoughts of their
posting to Amsterdam the following week, Monsieur and
Madame Rivière motored over flooded roads in torrential
rain to the Mount Maulin Hotel near Enniskerry. Some of
the roads were completely impassable and it took them over
two hours to make the twelve-mile journey from Ailesbury
Road.

Eileen Beatty phoned Margaret Hamilton-Reid telling her

that the plane had crashed and that she was driving out to the Mount Maulin Hotel – there was no other news.

'We went as quickly as we could,' Eileen Beatty later reported. 'It was about eight P.M. and at this stage we didn't know what had happened.' By the time Eileen Beatty reached the hotel, an ambulance from Dun Laoghaire had already arrived to bring Chantal, Andrée and Capitaine Habez to hospital.

'Eileen Beatty told me there was no point in my going out – there were local people searching,' recalled Margaret Hamilton-Reid. She waited for news with her aunt in Rathgar, not knowing 'if there were any alive'.

As fears rose of a possible catastrophe, a phalanx of emergency services – more than two dozen ambulances, several fire engines and cars, the chief of staff of the army and the chief of police – converged on the Mount Maulin Hotel.

In the kitchen, staff member Madge Carroll was kept busy making endless cups of tea.

A little bit of local knowledge, as everybody knew, went a long way. Bill Deely, fourth-year medical student, was relaxing with his friend Conor Hogan in Prosser's Bar in Enniskerry when a local garda came in. Bill Deely could pinpoint the time when they received word of the crash: 'It couldn't have been much later than 7 P.M. because we weren't nearly drunk.'

Bill and Conor knew every hill and hummock in the area – this was where they poached and they were familiar with all the little streams and rivulets that coursed their way down the rugged mountains. They were well used to hopping from stone to stone over rivers and clambering off trails to 'pull deer'. They also knew that the terrain could be very dangerous – 'one false step and you could go down up to your neck

very quickly'. In this rain, a dry sheep track could turn into a
brimming stream within seconds.

The garda asked Bill and Conor if they could suggest
what part of the mountain the plane might have come down
on 'because it was a big area and the girl wasn't able to give
any clear direction from where she'd come'.

Bill Deely and Conor Hogan quickly returned to Bill
Deely's house to pick up his father, the local doctor, and his
medical bag. Jumping into their car, they drove through
Ballinagee, where Norman Keegan the farmer, just in from
milking the cows, joined them. Further up the road at the
Mount Maulin Hotel they collected Brian Hogan.

'We decided the quickest way to the mountains was to go
by the Paddocks on the old Long Hill Road' – one of the
two roads between Roundwood and Enniskerry – wrote
Brian Hogan. 'When we arrived we were quickly joined by the
Enniskerry gardaí. We divided into parties for the search,
some heading for War Hill, others for Djouce.'

Bill Deely junior and senior, Norman Keegan and Conor
Hogan drove out to a point along the old Long Hill Road.
They parked the car outside 'Mulligans' house, under the
shadow of Mount Maulin'.

'We took up the valley between Mount Maulin and
Djouce and came to a river in flood. I was following the
"local doctor". I was carrying his bag,' explained Bill. It was
raining hard and Bill's father was falling behind. Bill had to
haul the doctor's bag over the swollen river. The young
medical student wasn't 'afraid of a bit of water'. Dr Deely
began to falter on the path. Unable to traverse the flooded
stream, the doctor left the two younger men to cross and
continue without him. 'We went up the valley between War
Hill and Djouce, following a wire fence. It was the fence
which gave us the clue.' They were following a track, probably
part of an ancient route from near Ballinastoe townland,
climbing the glen of the Stoney Pass River. The wire fencing

led north-west, dividing Ballinastoe from Glasnamullan, and marked the limits of Lord Powerscourt's properties.

'The fog was down to the ground. It would then lift for a bit and we would carry on.'

With the clouds hanging so low over the mountains, the Bray gardaí judged that there were less than three hours of daylight left, more like two. They left their station in search of further people who might be familiar with the area. Calling into the Bray Snooker Club they immediately found ten volunteers, including twenty-nine-year-old Pearce Kenny. Driving out to Enniskerry on their way to the Mount Maulin Hotel, they passed Paul Rowan, the seed merchant, in Bray Main Street, a young man whom one of the gardaí knew.

> We did a lot of shooting and fishing at that time and the guard stopped me in the lashing rain and said 'Paul, you know the mountains up there very well. We have word that there has been a plane crash. It could be somewhere round the Three Rock Mountain.'

A lucky car owner in those days of strict petrol rationing, Paul collected his brother Diarmuid and a friend, Ferdiad McKinney – son of Colonel McKinney, who had been instrumental in setting up the Irish Red Cross hospital in Saint Lô – and set off, heading south towards the Sally Gap along the Military Road.

> It was lashing. The rain had washed away bridges but we were lucky; we got over two or three of them where the water was nine or ten inches from the top of the tunnel. It seems like madness now but when you're a teenager you don't realise these problems.

As news of the calamity spread to surrounding townlands, other locals put together their collective knowledge. Norman Keegan's son Charlie rapidly changed into a new pair of gumboots and went to pick up Bill Hicks from the gate lodge at the Powerscourt Waterfall, and the forester Ashley Greig.

Ashley Greig, who knew the area as well as any of the locals, led the way.

'All we knew was that a plane had crashed. We didn't know if anyone was hurt or killed or anything,' said Charlie Keegan.

> We started up the mountain between Djouce and Maulin. There were others but I never came into contact with them. It was spitting out of the heavens — heavy rain, there were streams coming down off the mountains in torrents. You'd be afraid of your life to be swept away.

Others joined in the search — locals and emergency services combined. 'People were leaving in dribs and drabs, taking different routes in every conceivable direction.' Dan Nolan, another Enniskerry local, went out on horseback.

An army search party, under the command of General Hugo MacNeill, set off for Glencree to cover the area from the west, approaching the scene from the Military Road. They struck out in the direction of Tonduff. Ambulances started to congregate along the old Long Hill Road. The chief of police ordered a search party to cover the area around the Sally Gap. The mist was so thick and swirling, the driving rain so heavy, they could see only a few feet in front of them and small search groups would keep losing each other. At times, to stop themselves from being blown over, the searchers linked themselves together so they would not be separated or fall into hidden bog holes.

Hindered by the rain and the fog, many went astray. Others gave up, returning home soaked and exhausted. Defeated by the hostile elements, Charlie Keegan, Ashley Greig and Bill Hicks came down after two hours. 'We went up to the top of the mountain and we searched and searched. We couldn't find any trace of a plane.'

The chief aeronautical officer of the Department of Industry and Commerce, Mr Richard O'Sullivan, also failed to find any sign of a wreck. He had been informed that the plane had been out of communication with Dublin air-traffic control since about midday. Alerted to the crash at his home, he set off at once to the garda station in Enniskerry and then continued towards the ambulances and doctors in cars that had congregated on the old Long Hill Road. 'There were a large number of ambulance personnel proceeding along a track across the hillside carrying stretchers and blankets but I found that they had no idea as to the location of the aircraft.' Joining in the search, he recorded:

> Darkness was imminent when I got to the Rocky Valley ...
> I soon became hopelessly lost in the rugged terrain ... In
> the murky blackness I became aware of a dim figure of a
> man with a stick and a dog. I was happy to hail him and ask
> the way down.

The man turned out to be a local shepherd. 'He told me he'd been looking for a lost sheep. He had no knowledge of the crash.'

Three hours passed. The search continued as the last vestiges of daylight departed, giving way to grey dusk and a night of almost total blackness.

Twenty

With the help of *les trois valides*, Eliane, Monique and Antoinette Nattier, it took Lilette nearly six hours to separate the most seriously injured from the less badly off. She had enough medical knowledge to deduce that some of the girls had incurred serious fractures. Others had deep wounds. Any movement would risk exacerbating their condition. She could only try to make them as comfortable as possible in the cramped interior.

There were seven girls that she didn't want to move. Covering them with their own capes, propping their heads on folded jumpers or cushions from the upturned seats, the four least injured girls ignored their own pain and the cold that was beginning to turn their lips blue. They worked inside the damaged fuselage, water dripping through the roof, the door hanging from one hinge, flapping in the wind which continued to howl outside. They cleared pieces of turf and branches from on top of other girls. They picked their way where necessary over bodies. Occasionally they stopped and stared before resuming their tasks and sometimes they peered out of the cabin door at the endless rain and swirling cloud outside.

Geneviève was trapped beneath the floor, her legs

entangled in twisted pieces of metal. She felt pain. She didn't know whether it was dream pain or real pain. Micheline and Catherine winced at the slightest pressure on their legs. Nicole, sitting next to Micheline, became mesmerised by the drops of cold water falling into the wound in her knee. Magali drifted in and out of consciousness. When she awoke her head was pounding. Her throat was parched. Agnès lay as still as she could on her side, only half-aware of her surroundings. Anne Lemonnier was in a coma.

Four less-injured girls – Ginette Martin, Janine Alexandre, Odile Lecoquière and Odile Stahlberger – carefully and painfully extricated their limbs from their immobile companions and crawled to the back of the plane over oil, soiled luggage, broken seats and pieces of earth. Françoise, already near the rear of the fuselage, stayed where she was in a state of delirium, sitting next to the fire extinguisher. Blood dripping from the deep cut in her ankle, Antoinette Emo also pulled herself past the others to the rear of the plane.

And, since they did not know how long it would take for help to arrive, they somehow let their pain grow remote. They became immune to the falling temperature inside the fuselage, immune to their injuries. Time lost all meaning during the long hours that followed so that later they could not remember whether they had been awake or asleep.

Only Lilette took in the whole sorry picture and wondered at times if help would ever arrive and if it did would it be too late.

Lilette counted the girls. They were her girls now, her responsibility. She had nine at the back, including Sylvia and *les trois valides*, plus seven who could not be moved. But there was one other girl that she had not accounted for.

Sitting in the toilet was Jacqueline Conort. 'I was knocking on the door but nobody heard.'

Apart from the air hostess, who lay motionless, there was

no sign of the other members of the crew. The wireless operator, the navigator and the engineer had all left the plane. Shortly after the crash, Lilette remembered hearing a weak announcement: 'Be calm little girls, we will shortly be arriving in Dublin.' It had been the broken voice of the navigator, Michel Tourret, but when she looked inside the cockpit nobody was there. She gazed at multi-coloured cables, at switches, levers and gauges that must have meant something to an engineer but to her were unfathomable. A soiled map of the Irish Sea lay abandoned on the floor under the steering column, which was broken in two. In the wireless room, the Morse key had rolled onto the floor.

The Fancy Spoke,
Shiny rock hard slope
To the black depth of Lough Tay,
The mirrored mica beach, mossy rocks.

Moral oaks, bent branches in the ray
Of the clear blue sky,
Beauty shocks.
On the green expanse deer run, leap
In the wealth of nature.
Breath, weep
For joy in creation, created,
The hollow of sweet sounds, Luggala.

From 'Luggala – Hollow of Sweet Sounds'
Dominick Browne

Twenty-one

Enniskerry formed part of the Powerscourt Estate and Lord Powerscourt lived on his demesne in the magnificent Powerscourt House with its stunning Golden Gate and beautiful views of the Sugarloaf Mountain. From Enniskerry, the old mail-coach route, the original old Long Hill Road, headed through Ballinastoe towards Roundwood. On the right a badly maintained road, known locally as Murdering Pass or Murdering Steps, dipped and rose as it meandered towards the Sally Gap, passing above a ridge that looked down on the shooting lodge of Luggala.

Luggala, which meant 'the hollow of sweet sounds', nestled on the banks of Lough Tay. Built in 1790 by Mr La Touche, a prominent banker, it later passed into the hands of Lord Powerscourt. The house, which stood on seven thousand acres of land, was sold by Lord Powerscourt to the famous Guinness brewery family and had been a wedding present from Ernest Guinness to his daughter Oonagh when she married Lord Oranmore and Browne, her second husband, in 1936.

For a 'big house' it was relatively modest and somewhat spartan.

'There were five bedrooms upstairs all of which had

different names,' remarked Dominick Browne, Lord Oranmore's eldest son by his first marriage: the single shamrock room, the double shamrock room, the night nursery, the passage room – so called because everybody had to pass through it to reach the other rooms – and the top room. Two tin baths stood in one bathroom. The plumbing creaked and the water ran brown and cold from the rusty taps.

Oonagh later converted the large room downstairs – known as the dormitory – into a dining-room. The house then became famous for its rakish parties with large groups of artists and writers. Often more than thirty people stayed the night. 'Nothing but foie gras and Bloody Marys for breakfast. It was an age that cannot be repeated,' wrote Oonagh's biographer, Kenneth Rose. Paul Rowan, the seed merchant's son, remembered being at some of them. 'They went on all night. We had breakfast before I went home at five in the morning. They were extraordinary days.'

However, in 1946 the house was used less frequently. During the summer, the children used to come over to Ireland from their boarding-schools in England or Scotland, spend three weeks at Castle MacGarrett, Lord Oranmore's ancestral home in County Mayo, and move on to Luggala for two or three weeks in August. Lord Oranmore, well liked by the staff on the estate in Castle MacGarrett, on account of his quiet good manners, always brought Cummins the butler and May the maid from Mayo to Wicklow.

A spacious living-room downstairs commanded a view of the steep, dark granite mountain known as the Fancy Rock. The mountain towered perpendicularly above Lough Tay and was mirrored in the lake's black peaty waters. At 1,957 feet, the lake is said to be as deep as the Fancy Rock is high, although this must be a fanciful claim. Small bog trout were found in abundance in the lake and young Dominick recalled catching sixty on a single day. Sitting in their boat, he and his father would cast their lines into the deep water using the golden Wickham's Fancy fly.

Deer grazed in the parkland, which was dotted with oak and ash trees. 'Fancy' meant the 'rock of ash trees'. It was the only wooded area in an otherwise treeless region and the green floor of the valley ran down to the bright, sandy beach of the lake. On the far side of Lough Tay, the River Cloghoge wound its way through the valley to Lough Dan.

'You could look down into the valley through the trees,' remarked Pa Brennan, 'and I'd sometimes see Oonagh sunning herself on the lawn, although "he" was no picture.'

A noted beauty, Oonagh was the youngest daughter of Ernest Guinness. 'With large doe-like eyes, shining hair, pale arms, social position and, of course, money, his three daughters, Aileen, Maureen and Oonagh, were collectively known as the Golden Guinness Girls. They were the true-life prototypes of the "It" crowd of the twenties. Oonagh was known as the nice one, kinder to her children and more generous than her sisters,' recorded *The Sunday Times*.

Oonagh's husband, Lord Oranmore, on the other hand, was far less glamorous looking and was short of stature and stocky in build.

Born in Dublin in 1901, Dominick Geoffrey Edward Browne was the eldest son of the third Lord Oranmore and Browne and his wife Olwen, whose origins went back to the feudal tribes of medieval Galway. *Foriter et Fideliter* (strongly and faithfully) was the family motto.

The early part of his life was spent between the three-thousand-acre estate at Castle MacGarrett in Mayo, Mereworth Castle in Kent and Belgravia in London.

Lord Oranmore, whose nickname was Dom-Dom, was immune to what people thought of him, according to his son, and did not hold any strong religious beliefs. However, his quiet sense of humour made him popular in his circle — one of the many stories he recounted was of a local pastor with a lisp who would end his sermons with the solemn pronouncement: 'God shave the Queen.'

'He didn't care very much about anything,' his son Dominick said. 'He was convinced that there was no God and that life was pretty pointless really. Just before he died in London at the age of one hundred, a specialist doctor was summoned from Dublin to his bedside. "Lord Oranmore, do you believe in God?"' the doctor asked, to which his father replied, '"Sometimes." That was the extent of it.'

During the Second World War he had professed sympathy with the Germans, a not uncommon stance within the aristocracy at the time. Whether because of this or that he was thirty-eight years old when war broke out, he was refused admission to the British army. He joined the Local Defence Force instead and considered himself an Irishman.

He was catapulted into his father's position when both his parents were killed in a motorcar accident when he was twenty-five years old. It was the beginning of a life that would be marred by tragedy.

August 1946 brought more sadness. The sudden death of Oonagh's daughter (by her first marriage), Tessa Kindersley, a vivacious fourteen-year-old, after a diphtheria injection, cast a pall over the family that summer. A well-known winner of jumping competitions at the Dublin Horse Show, her 'tiny figure, long golden hair flying in the breeze, a bowler hat on the back of her head', had attracted much attention as she did her clear rounds over the courses seven years before at Ballsbridge. A few hours before her death, Tessa had been schooling a recently acquired Connemara pony for the show.

'The overhanging Wicklow Hills, the sparkling waters of Lough Tay and the fresh green fronds of bracken seemed to be fitting guardians for the resting place of Tessa, symbolising as they do, her determination, her brightness, which covered a real depth of character and her boundless energy,' began the appreciation in *The Irish Times* on 8 August.

On 12 August, a shooting party would have been common on the opening day of the grouse season. Lord Oranmore and Browne was once said to be the finest shot in Ireland. The Irish record of a 221 grouse killing in one day had been set in the grounds of Luggala. But in 1946, there is no record of any group gathering at the house for the opening of the season – the visitors' book only recording members of the family present. Young Dominick was in the house, as was his brother Martin who signed the visitors' book that day. According to Dominick their half-brothers, baby Tara, born the year before, and Garech Browne, just seven years old, together with cousin Olwen and Gay Kindersley, Oonagh's son from her first marriage, were also at the house.

At eight o'clock the family sat down to dinner in the living-room on, Dominick recalled, 'quite uncomfortable chairs', the seats of which were 'made out of horsehair which stuck into you'.

At about nine in the evening – at least two hours after Chantal de Vitry had stumbled into the front hall of the Mount Maulin Hotel seven miles away – Lord Oranmore and Browne was about to read the day's papers when Dominick said they were astonished to see two young men in uniform stagger across the lawn. It was just after the war and for a second they thought they were Germans on the run.

Some moments later, there was the sound of voices – raised, anxious – and then urgent knocking.

Cummins the butler opened the door to navigator Michel Tourret and wireless operator Daniel Duran, neither of whom could speak a word of English. In considerable distress, the two bedraggled Frenchmen stood on the gravel under the double heads of the stone eagle that perched above the door, desperately trying to explain their plight. Although there was no phone in the house at the time – it was only later, in 1951, that the Minister for Posts and

Communications, Lord Oranmore's neighbour and friend Erskine Childers, arranged for the telephone wires to be brought from Roundwood to Luggala – Lord Oranmore had a car and he spoke French rather well.

An hour later, five miles away, Pat O'Brien, dressed in his LDF uniform, came out of Keenan's Hotel in the village of Roundwood, which in those days was used for local LDF meetings. Chatting with his friend Criostoir Byrne in the rain, he was surprised to see a Ford V8 Station Wagon pull up beside them with Lord Oranmore and Browne, dressed in a Burberry coat, at the wheel.

The forty-six-year-old squire – not noted for mixing with the locals – wound down the window and the two Roundwood men greeted him deferentially. Lord Oranmore and Browne boomed, in what Pat O'Brien described as 'his lovely Oxford accent', 'Are you coming to the rescue?'

They didn't have a clue what he was talking about.

Nevertheless, Pat O'Brien and Criostoir Byrne got willingly into the car with the man from the big house. 'We wouldn't query him. We looked up to him. He had married Oonagh Guinness and the Guinnesses were great employers.' On hearing the story of the Frenchmen stumbling into Luggala from a stricken plane, Pat O'Brien suggested to Lord Oranmore that the two members of the crew might have followed the stream known locally as the Piper's Brook, which flowed down Djouce Mountain and under the Boleyhorrigan Bridge.

'How do you know the district so well?' asked Lord Oranmore, genuinely impressed. The river flowed through his property and passed near the gable end of his house before entering Lough Tay.

'We were on the turf all during the war years,' replied Pat O'Brien, omitting to mention that the area was also where many of the locals poached.

Driving to the spot along the Sally Gap Road, they parked the Woody Station Wagon near the Boleyhorrigan Bridge. 'Can you imagine leaving your car there today? It wouldn't be there for long,' added Pat O'Brien. The three men set off following the Piper's Brook using Lord Oranmore's torch to guide them. 'The fog and the rain was something inhuman,' Pat O' Brien recalled.

As the unremitting weather continued, the Sally Gap Road started to fill with more cars and lorries. News of the accident quickly spread round the village of Roundwood and into its surroundings. The young and the strong joined together in small groups and headed to the part of the road above Luggala. W.S. Doyle's turf lorry carried some of the men, driven by Michael Rooney. Fred Doyle drove his butcher's van – the place was inundated with Doyles, Timmonses and quite a few Brennans too. Pa Brennan drove out in his own car with his friend Paddy Brennan. Pa's brother Anthony Brennan jumped onto one of the lorries.

Sergeant McNally took over the coordination of the rescue operation from the Roundwood side. McNally also understood that these locals had walked and walked the hills and knew the area inside out.

Sergeant McNally had been at Roundwood station since August 1942, having served in Mullingar, Galway and Kells. Well liked and respected by the locals, the fifty-four-year-old garda took a pragmatic approach to policing. 'He knew we were doing it. But he also knew I couldn't be summoned for shooting deer because', said Pa Brennan, 'deer were considered vermin at that time. The place was overrun with them.'

It wasn't long before McNally had a posse of lads eager and willing to work under his command: Matt Keenan, Jimmy Price, Ned Curley, Jimmy Kavanagh, Pat Hughes,

Peter Hatton, Mick Hayes, Willie Rooney, Paddy Doyle, Jack Brennan, Bill Kenna and Billy Brien to name but some mentioned in the local paper, the *Wicklow People*.

People now were converging on the mountains from all different directions: from Enniskerry in the north, Roundwood to the south, the old Long Hill Road to the east and Glencree and the Sally Gap in the west, but few sounds were heard beyond the occasional squawks of the black ravens above the Fancy Rock, though, by this time, there must have been a hundred or so men moving about within an eight-square-mile area. They were men with a job to do. Ignoring the wind and the rain, they made their way towards the same area, drawn by a common instinct.

The great mountains – Tonelagee, Mullaghcleavaun, Duff Hill, Gravale, Kippure, Tonduff, War Hill, Maulin and Djouce – mountains that the locals knew better than their own backyards, seemed like one mighty, desolate mass in the dense fog and mist.

At 10.30 P.M. Enniskerry lads Bill Deely and Conor Hogan stopped for a smoke. They had spent over three hours combing the area in the pouring rain with local farmer Norman Keegan and were on the point of turning back for home. It is very much colder at two thousand feet than at sea level. A breeze on the low ground is a strong wind higher up. The wind stung their faces. The clouds occasionally parted, only to be swallowed up in an instant.

'Suddenly the fog lifted momentarily and we could see the plane not twenty yards away,' recalled Bill Deely. 'It was rather provident.'

As daylight faded, the ghost-like outline of the Junkers 52 appeared on the side of the mountain looking almost intact.

Moments later it vanished again in the thick mist as if it had been a mirage.

Twenty-two

In the blackness torches gathered.

Sylvia screamed, 'The rescuers are here!' After more than ten hours of waiting, Janine heard a sound outside. 'I can still hear the cries of joy in the plane.'

Looking out of the porthole in the dark, Micheline first saw the dim light of a torch. The light grew brighter. She heard voices and shouts. The light moved into the cabin and illuminated the roof, the sides and the floor of the plane. And in that light, much was revealed.

As she drifted in and out of consciousness, for Sylvia only two images stayed in her mind between bits of splintered conversation. The first image was of the horror of the immediate aftermath of the crash, 'of blood and engine oil everywhere. It was dirty and cold. The floor had opened up and I had fallen through.' The second 'was of this leg. It was the trouser leg of a local man – *un paysan*. I held the leg of this man as tightly as I could and I wouldn't let him go – he was my salvation.'

Bill Deely, carrying his father's medical bag, was the first to climb in through the open door of the plane. While Conor Hogan retraced his steps, according to one report, 'blowing a whistle' – a Girl Guide's whistle – down the mountain, Bill Deely set to work, drawing on his four years of medical-studies experience.

Alerted by Conor Hogan, Sergeant Wickham from Enniskerry and Sergeant Kelly drawn in from the Baltinglass station climbed up to the site of the crash, directed by the local Enniskerry postman, James Doran. It took them about two hours by the shortest route. They sent up flares and they flashed torches from the summit of Djouce Mountain.

Tante Ju, another nickname for which was *Iron Annie*, had ploughed over a ridge, slewing round to the right before coming to rest on the south-west shoulder of Djouce. *Corrugated Coffin* was the Junkers' other nickname and only yards away, an ancient rock known as the coffin stone lay on the saddle separating Djouce from War Hill.

Dominating the skyline between Roundwood and Enniskerry, Djouce, pronounced 'jowse', was the principal mountain in the Glencree chain, reaching a height of 2,385 feet. While it was not the highest mountain in Wicklow, it could certainly claim to be the biggest, with many deceptive hillocks. The origin of its name is uncertain – it was variously called Dewys, Duce, Douce and Dubh Ais. The last of these meant 'black back' and, looking from the Deerpark, it appeared as a great, dark pyramid.

One theory was that a family named Douce lived there hundreds of years ago but it is far more likely that the family took its name from the mountain rather than the other way round.

It may also have been named after the goddess Digais, who featured in an early bardic poem, 'Bairend Chermain', dating back to at least the eleventh century. One of the five daughters of Digais was called Malu and this could have been the name for Mount Maulin to the north. The identification of Digais with Djouce was also supported by the line of the poem, 'Digais lived on her mountain.' Leitrim, the old name for Roundwood, appeared earlier on in the poem as Liathdruim.

It has been suggested that another meaning of the name Djouce is 'di-chois', which translates as 'not to be travelled over by foot'.

Walkers had often become lost on the mountain in the past when great sweeping clouds came rushing towards them, blotting everything else out of sight. Published in the *Belfast Magazine and Literary Journal* of 1825 and reproduced in Michael Fewer's book *A Walk in Ireland*, a traveller called 'G', in the summer of 1843, attempted to walk, with a female companion, from Luggala, then owned by the banker La Touche, to the Powerscourt demesne near Enniskerry – being advised to ascend Djouce, 'as this would both shorten the road and give us a magnificent view from the summit of Douce'.

> We were also directed to call at the house of Mr La Touche's shepherd who would show us the way over the mountain ... she accompanied us nearly to the top of the mountain and pointed out our way, but not long after she left us, there came a mist so thick that we could not distinguish objects a few yards distant. After wandering some time under this mist, I felt considerable uneasiness lest we should fall into some bog or over some precipice. We were indeed in a perilous state for nearly three hours, a time greatly more sufficient to reach the bottom of the hill, which I imagined we had crossed. Still there appeared no termination to our toils and dangers; now we met a swamp, which we were obliged to go around, then a torrent overhung by almost impassable rocks, which we were compelled to cross. The fortitude of my fellow traveller forsook at last, and after suffering above three hours of terror, she cried out in a voice of joy, 'There is a cottage chimney' – but it was the horn of a cow! We experienced many such delusions, and after wandering among quagmires and precipices of this mountain, a sunbeam burst from the

cloud, and showed us a little cabin glittering at no great distance. It was again almost instantaneously hid from our sight, yet I marked the place and we soon reached it, when to my astonishment, a hoarse laugh was raised, and a voice cried out in a tone of triumph, 'Did I not tell you, you could never cross the mountain?' This salutation I could not understand till looking around me for a moment, I observed that we were in the very shepherd's cabin we had left between three and four hours before.

Of all the mountains in the area, none had such an extensive cushion of heather and moss. Reaching up to the thighs in places, it made walking difficult even in good weather. Hidden bog holes added to the hazardous nature of the terrain. However, hundreds of years ago, in pre-Christian times, a track leading up to the summit of the mountain from the crossroads in Ballinastoe was said to be part of a pilgrim's route and amongst the locals the tradition still exists that Djouce was a sacred mountain. It was near to this ancient path that Bill Deely and Conor Hogan had probably walked to reach what some people would later call a 'modern-day miracle'.

Twenty-three

As the flares shone from the top of the mountain, Bill Deely set about segregating those that needed stretchering. 'There were some fairly deep wounds. I pulled them together to tide them over so that there was no haemorrhaging,' he said. 'I also splinted a few broken legs and arms.' Although he had morphine in his bag he didn't use it. Being only a student doctor, he 'wasn't entitled to and in those days you adhered to the regulations'.

Alerted to a persistent tapping inside the cabin, he opened the toilet door and Jacqueline Conort fell out, eyes wide with anguish. Her face was covered with cuts and bruises but she had been saved from more serious leg injuries by the rubber soles of her sandals. 'He bound my legs together with heather. It hurt a lot,' she remembered.

Approaching from the Sally Gap side, Paul Rowan's brother Diarmuid was the first to spot a light – a tiny spark almost buried in the dark – flashing on top of the mountain. It could have been a fire or a lamp. Paul, Diarmuid and Ferdiad McKinney set off for this 'occasionally flashing light'.

'And to our horror – you see we thought the light was only

a mile away – we went up a quarter of a mile and didn't the mountain dip, go way down and up again? We could do nothing about that. It was bucketing down with a high wind and black dark.'

They eventually spotted the badly damaged plane. 'It was full of young girls all speaking French in a very excited way. There were many tears.'

From what he could see, the injuries were superficial. The men tore up their white shirts – the only parts they didn't need to tear were the sleeves – and used them as bandages.

> We came across this girl who had a terrible pain in her arm, her leg and on her left side and we cut some thick branches of heather – everybody carried knives in those days – and strapped them to her leg. We bound it with one of our ties but then we had no way of getting her down because we hadn't got stretchers. The door of the plane was hanging off so we tore it down and put her on the door and started to go down the mountain – the three of us. She would say things in French, such as, 'Je suis tombée à gauche.' So we would reverse the procedure so that she was lying on her right hand side.

Paul Rowan had no recollection of any other rescuers. 'We got there first. There was nobody else there.'

As the news gradually spread that the plane had been located on Djouce Mountain, on the south-west side, the focus of the rescue operation shifted from Enniskerry in the north to Roundwood on the other side of the mountain.

Ambulances, fire engines, doctors and nurses battled once again through flooded roads and atrocious conditions to get to points on the road as close as physically possible to the scene of the accident.

Amongst these were Monsieur and Madame Rivière and Eileen Beatty. Eileen Beatty later reported: 'About 10.30 P.M. we learned that the plane had been found. Ambulances set off from the Mount Maulin Hotel into the mountains and I was able to board one of them.' By midnight, having travelled over very bad roads and mountain tracks, she still had another three miles to cover before reaching the scene of the crash.

Following the stream, Lord Oranmore, Pat O'Brien and Criostoir Byrne eventually reached the end of the Piper's Brook. The fog made it impossible to see which direction they were going in. 'We followed the river up about half-way where it branches off to the right, then instead of turning to the right we continued on up straight. The higher up the mountain we went the denser the fog became.' After some time they found one of the wheels of the plane, which had separated from the rest of the aircraft.

'The huge wheel was still inflated and it could have travelled a long way.' They heard a whistling sound. It turned out to be 'the wind blowing through the struts of the wings of the plane'. Half an hour after finding the wheel, they finally reached the crash site. 'We could hear the girls inside the plane moaning and talking.

'The whole place around the wreckage was saturated with fuel and the engine oil was six inches deep.' Lord Oranmore, according to Pat O'Brien, shouted, 'No matches or cigarettes!' He then climbed into the wreck of the aircraft, shining his torch on the girls one by one.

Pat O'Brien continued:

> He said to me, pointing, 'She looks in a bad way, we'll try and get her down.' Her face and neck were in a terrible state. I caught her hand and put her over my shoulder. She was completely motionless but we were holding her hand and I could feel the regular beat of her pulse. That's the only way I knew she was alive.
>
> We must have fallen a hundred times coming down the mountain. We would try to get her up and we'd then fall again. It took us two hours to get down the mountain with Lord Oranmore coming down beside us — it was a hell of a walk. He did not carry anyone on his back. He did not

indeed. He wouldn't have had a partner you see. We lost our way in the black dark and fog and ended up on the road a mile away from where we had started.

Attracted by Sergeant Wickham's flares from the top of Djouce, Pa Brennan and Paddy Brennan finally reached the wreck of the plane. They pulled out one of the least injured girls, asking if she could walk.

'It took well over an hour to get down,' remembered Pa Brennan, 'falling into holes three or four feet deep and full of water.' The water squelched in their boots. Taking turns, the two strong men lifted the girl onto their shoulders and followed the stream down to the road. Ahead of them, other survivors were making the same long, slow, difficult journey down. Picking their way in the darkness, they could see virtually nothing. The uneven ground had been torn up by the storm. Every few yards their path was blocked by fallen rocks, boulders, displaced mounds of earth and floods.

'We had a job to do and we got on with it,' said Pa Brennan. 'You had to do something; it was an unspoken thing.'

The girl laughed at times on the precarious journey down, which Pa Brennan observed 'can sometimes happen at times of stress'. Laughter: the antidote to fear.

The least injured were shepherded down the mountain first, towards Luggala, in the direction of Roundwood, which was by far the shortest route to the road. It was the opposite direction to that taken by Chantal, Andrée and the pilot.

First to be brought down were the three uninjured girls, Monique, Eliane and Antoinette Nattier.

'After eleven hours of this nightmare, three Irishmen arrived with torches and they asked those who could walk to go down the mountain with them,' said Monique. 'The rescuers with stretchers had not arrived yet.'

'We went down a mountain and passed streams,' remembered Eliane. 'I was on this man's back, covered in his overcoat.'

'I had a great pain in my ankle which turned out to be twisted so this brave local lifted me on his back and we fell several times into holes,' added Monique.

The slow descent down the mountain, hindered by the weather, put the rescuers and the rescued at risk. In the wind, cold, rain and mist, without proper protective clothing or stout boots, they fell several times. It took more than two hours to bring *les trois valides* to the safety of the road and the waiting ambulances.

'Then, in the dark night, I finally left the machine with a member of the emergency services,' remembered Odile Lecoquière. 'I confirmed that I could walk and was held up by somebody. I stumbled and fell all the time – into bog holes.'

'That one's sleeping.' Françoise felt two slaps on her face. 'I had the impression that I was walking in mud. Somebody on the right-hand side was supporting me but the person holding my left arm kept stumbling.'

From the villages of Roundwood, Enniskerry and Newtown Mount Kennedy, from Dublin, Greystones and Bray, members of the community from all walks of life were gradually converging on the scene of the accident.

It was reported that William Fitzsimmons, chief engineer of Roundwood Reservoir, struggled up the mountain with the first food for the girls. Mademoiselle d'Harcourt and Mademoiselle de la Motte, French teachers at the Red Cross hostel at Glencree, waded knee-deep up the slopes and were the first women to reach the plane. A sales representative for Clubman Shirts, thirty-eight-year-old Dennis Dorgan, and an Italian charcoal burner arrived at the roadside and toiled up the hostile hill to give what help they could.

Father Eugene Doherty and Father Michael Keohane

from Glencree motored across the mountains over partly caved-in roads and eventually reached the plane 'to give spiritual aid to the victims'. They carried a small leather packet containing a pyx with hosts, oil and six pieces of cotton. 'Both of us considered it our duty to be there ... to alleviate to the best of our ability the sufferings of the French children who had such a terrifying experience.' *Per istam sanctam Unctionem et suam piissimam misericordiam indulgeat tibi Dominus quidquid per gressum deliquisti* – Through this blessed unction may the Lord pardon thee whatever sins or faults you have committed.

Feu, feux, s.m. Fire
Follet, a. Merry, lively
Feu follet, will-o'-the-wisp

In Ireland the will-o'-the-wisp is associated with ghostly apparitions. One event in the fifties attracted busloads of the curious from all over the country. Some thought it was the Virgin Mary appearing. My father said he saw it high up in the pine trees. One local fell down a bog hole as she ran after the elusive dancing lights.

Billy Doran

Twenty-four

Geneviève lay as still as she could and listened. Then the storm abated.

The rescue operation continued through the night and it wasn't until about one in the morning that the army, under the command of Major General Hugo MacNeill, finally got through with stretchers.

Bill Deely helped to lift the badly injured onto the stretchers, which were each carried by four men. It was time for Catherine, Magali, Micheline, Nicole, Geneviève and Anne to be brought down the mountain. When the stretcher-bearers arrived, Janine was still in the plane, though most of the 'walking wounded' had now been shepherded down to safety.

> I was practically the last to leave, at the same time as two of the most seriously injured. I remember very clearly a feeling of well-being when I was laid out on the stretcher, under the thick blankets. I began to get warm despite the external cold of the night. What a relief to be looked after by such solid, strong bearers.

At some point, she was given a hot drink, a cup of 'milky sugared tea'. 'I have never tasted anything so good in my life.'

Suddenly this frightening moment was transformed into one of her sweetest memories.

'Then it was the descent – how difficult it was for these men, so loaded down with the stretcher, having to go forward on wet, bumpy ground and to walk off tracks in the night towards the valley.'

Nicole was one of the last to be taken down. In the small hours of the morning she was lifted clear of the metal that had trapped her damaged knee and lowered onto a stretcher. Lying horizontal, she saw the thin sliver of the moon shining palely through the cloud. On her downward journey, with the men manoeuvring her as gently as possible over the uneven ground, Nicole gazed up through a rift in the sky and could see the misty Milky Way. Gradually the sky turned into a great black bowl above her, pierced with stars. As she lay on her back, swaying from side to side, they twinkled and trembled. She had earned a badge (*un brevet*) in astronomy and was able to pick out the constellations one by one: the Plough, the Great Bear and the brightest of all the stars, the North Star. Vast Orion, with his shining belt, strode across the calm sky. The stars were like leaves, blowing in the wind. She tried to concentrate on all of them and on the infinite distance above her.

She thought she was going to die of thirst. But for her, no hot milky tea was forthcoming. In execrable English she asked the rescuers for something to drink but all that they heard was, 'I am dirty.'

The transport down the mountain is also Micheline's most vivid memory – 'on stretchers lit by resin torches, burning in the night'.

After four paramedics had cut her out of the tangled metal and lifted her slowly onto a stretcher, Geneviève remembered another form of light as the men picked their way over the soggy ground in the dark. It was a flashing, phosphorescent sort of glow, which seemed to come from the earth itself. Antoinette Emo also saw the flickering lights, the *feux follets* — will-o'-the-wisps — like jack-o'-lanterns hovering and slipping beneath them as they lay on the stretchers, which almost touched the ground but never quite did. As soon as one fire went out, or was swallowed by the mist, another lit up. There were at least twenty luminous dots zig-zagging over the land. They may have come from the torches or from the marsh gas formed by the chemical and physical interactions of decaying organic matter. Or perhaps they were reflections from ancient hidden treasures, the bottomless cache of artefacts preserved through time in the ancient bog.

And in case the rescuers should go astray, there was a suggestion of some guiding force, something beyond their understanding or that they had yet to grasp. It was as if the grim mountain was giving up its secrets, the spirits winking in the night at these last survivors to be brought down the wet slope of Djouce.

Shortly after Geneviève was carried away, the moon cast a silver stripe over the empty plane.

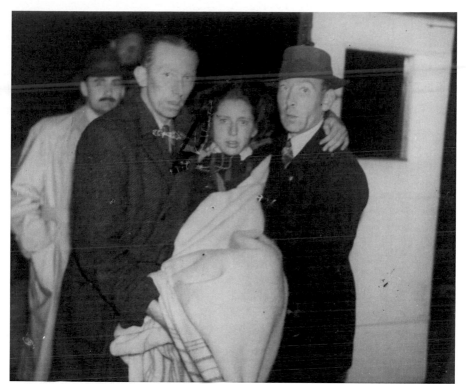

Locals lift one of the survivors into an ambulance. *Courtesy of Ministère des affairs étrangères - Nantes, Dublin (consulat, légation puis ambassade), article 121, dossier accident de l'avion < Junker 46 > dans le Wicklow le 12 août 1946.*

Antoinette Emo and Agnès Laporte (right) in an ambulance. *Courtesy of Ministère des affairs étrangères - Nantes, Dublin (consulat, légation puis ambassade), article 121, dossier accident de l'avion < Junker 46 > dans le Wicklow le 12 août 1946.*

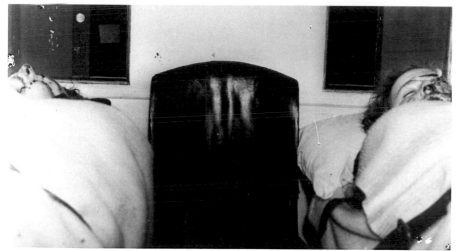

A shorn-off wheel of the Junkers 52 with the Great Sugarloaf in the background. *Courtesy of Ministère des affairs étrangères - Nantes, Dublin (consulat, légation puis ambassade), article 121, dossier accident de l'avion < Junker 46 > dans le Wicklow le 12 août 1946.*

Interior of the Junkers 52 after the crash. *Courtesy of Ministère des affairs étrangères - Nantes, Dublin (consulat, légation puis ambassade), article 121, dossier accident de l'avion < Junker 46 > dans le Wicklow le 12 août 1946.*

Views of the crashed Junkers 52. *Courtesy of Ministère des affairs étrangères - Nantes, Dublin (consulat, légation puis ambassade), article 121, dossier accident de l'avion < Junker 46 > dans le Wicklow le 12 août 1946.*

Margaret Hamilton-Reid c. 1946.
Courtesy of Margaret Hamilton-Reid.

Eileen Beatty, Secretary of The Irish Girl Guides, 1946. *Courtesy of The Irish Girl Guides.*

Pa Brennan in 1946. *Courtesy of Pa Brennan.*

The former Mount Maulin Hotel.
Author's photograph.

Luggala. *Author's photograph.*

Lord Oranmore and Browne c. 1946.
Courtesy of Dominick Browne.

Lady Oranmore and Browne (Oonagh Guinness) atop Lord Oranmore's
Ford V8 Woody Station Wagon in the forties. *Courtesy of Dominick Browne.*

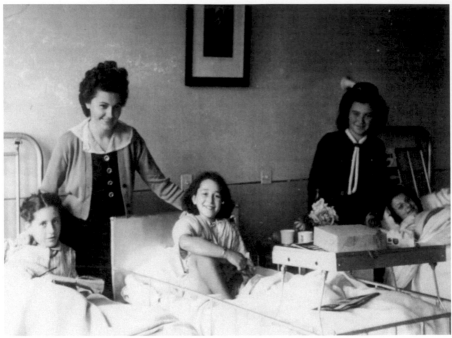

St Michael's Hospital, 1946. Left to right: Odile Stahlberger, Andrée Bonnet, Sylvia Ostrowetsky, Chantal de Vitry, Anne Lemonnier. *Courtesy of Geneviève Carrière.*

St Michael's Hospital, 1946. Agnès Laporte (in bed), Odile Lecoquière and Chantal de Vitry. *Courtesy of Geneviève Carrière.*

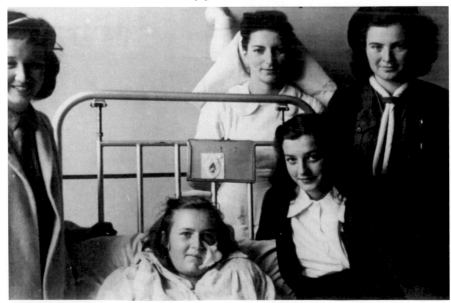

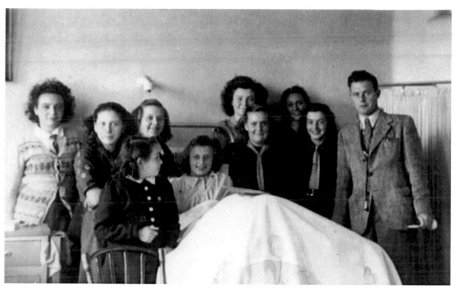

St Michael's Hospital, 1946. Left to right: Françoise Béchet, Odile Stahlberger, Sylvia Ostrowetsky, Janine Alexandre, Anne Lemmonier (in bed), Chantal de Vitry, Agnès Laporte, Ginette Martin, Odile Lecoquière, Dr Meagher. *Courtesy of Odile Longour.*

Dr Meagher and Geneviève Bétrancourt in St Michael's Hospital, 1946. *Courtesy of Geneviève Carrière.*

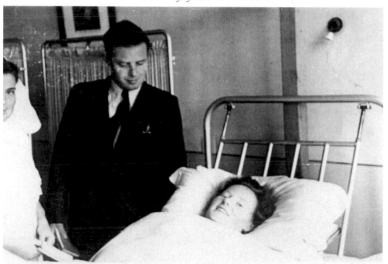

Above: Dutch and Irish Girl Guides at St Columba's College, Rathfarnham, 1946. *Courtesy of Muriel Webster.*

Left: *Les trois valides* arrive by car at the Rathfarnham camp, greeted by the camp Quartermaster, Doris Findlater, 1946. *Courtesy of Olive McKinley.*

Les trois valides at the Rathfarnham camp, 1946. Left to right: Monique Ygouf, Eliane Lemmonier and Antoinette Nattier with Estelle Moore (Group Commandant) and Lilette Levy-Bruhl. *Courtesy of Nicole Lucquin.*

Janine and Sylvia at the dog show in Dun Laoghaire, 1946. *Courtesy of Geneviève Carrière.*

'Farewell to Ireland', 9 September 1946. Left to right: Janine Alexandre, Françoise Béchet, Sylvia Ostrowetsky, Agnès Laporte, Odile Lecoquière, Odile Stahlberger. Madame Bétrancourt (mother of Geneviève) in head-scarf behind the wing of the plane. *Courtesy of Odile Longour.*

Above: Eleven *rescapées* return to Dublin, 1998. Left to right: Jacqueline (Conort), Catherine (de Geuser), Lilette (Levy-Bruhl), Andrée (Bonnet), Agnès (Laporte), Monique (Ygouf), Geneviève (Bétrancourt), Antoinette (Emo), Odile (Lecoquière), Chantal (de Vitry). In front: Nicole (Jacques-Léon). *Courtesy of Geneviève Carrière.*

Les rescapées return to Djouce Mountain, 1998. *Courtesy of Geneviève Carrière.*

'Dr Meagher's Girls' are reunited, 1998. Left to right: Chantal, Geneviève, Dr Meagher, Anne, Antoinette (Emo). *Courtesy of Geneviève Carrière.*

Ward One, St Bricin's Hospital, 1998. Left to right: Jacqueline, Antoinette (Emo), Nicole, Lilette and Catherine. *Courtesy of Geneviève Carrière.*

Crashed Junkers on Djouce Mountain, 13 August 1946. *Courtesy of Ministère des affairs étrangères -Nantes, Dublin (consulat, légation puis ambassade), article 121, dossier accident de l'avion < Junker 46 > dans le Wicklow le 12 août 1946.*

Author with part of the undercarriage, on Djouce Mountain, 12 August 2003. *Author's photograph.*

Twenty-five

Even those who could not recall their precarious journey down the mountain remembered the comforting warmth and glow of the big turf fire in the Sheepbank House.

The old stone hut on the Luggala estate was reached by a rough track from the main house, which ran up to the road. Dominick Browne recalled often taking walks along the stony path to the house during the holidays. It had once been inhabited by a family called Fanning – but had long since been derelict. It was from here that the unfortunate traveller 'G' had unsuccessfully set off across the mountains to reach the Powerscourt demesne in 1843. It was also the nearest sheltered area to the crash scene.

Oonagh (Lady Oranmore and Browne) set about converting the hut into a temporary refuge for the survivors and rescuers and a first-aid station for the medical teams. With the help of young Dominick, Cummins the butler, May the maid and various gardeners and gillies, she managed to get two big fires going. 'Lady Oranmore sent up her staff and they had brought up bedding and dry turf,' recalled Pat O'Brien.

They lit one fire inside the hut. This provided warmth and light for the doctors, nurses of the Red Cross and St John

Ambulance personnel to work by. It also provided a stove on which to brew tea. The other fire outside the hut on the road acted as a beacon to the rescuers. The locals said it was a marvel how they got those two fires going on such a dreadful, 'unreal' night.

For the children of Lord and Lady Oranmore it seemed like a big adventure. 'We thought it was all very exciting,' remembered Dominick. His cousin Olwen complained when told she had to stay in the big house and young Garech was put to bed.

The little cabin on the edge of the Guinness estate remains one of the strongest images in the minds of the girls when they think of their salvation. Cold water trickled down its moss-covered, slimy walls. It smelled of wet stone and damp earth. And yet it was converted into a sanctuary almost as welcoming as the Mount Maulin Hotel. For the injured girls – Agnès, Nicole, Sylvia, Catherine, Micheline, Magali and Ginette – the glimmer of the fire, the odour of burning turf and the warming drinks restored their hope and symbolised the end of their ordeal.

As the first girls were brought in, teeth chattering, they were revived with hot tea, whiskey and French brandy: brandy recently arrived on the same vessel, the SS *Penestin*, that had transported turf briquettes to Saint Lô the previous week.

Les trois valides arrived first. Eliane Lemonnier, like many of the others, had her first taste of whiskey there, which 'turned out to be very reviving'. Taking it neat from the bottle, the 'heat' from the whiskey is an image that Monique Ygouf will always keep and its medicinal warmth coursed right through her perished body.

Shortly after Father O'Hare from Newtown Mount Kennedy anointed her, Catherine de Geuser was brought round with a bottle under her nose. She retained a taste for a drop of Irish whiskey ever after.

Monsieur and Madame Rivière, the Minister to France and his wife, were among the first people to reach the hut. They spoke to Antoinette Nattier, taking her name and promising to let her parents know what had happened by telegram. They assured her they would tell them that she was unharmed.

Janine also met Monsieur Rivière, who came to speak to *les pauvres sœurs* – the little ones.

> This gentleman had occasion to render me a personal service. When leaning over my stretcher he asked me if I needed anything. Oh yes, I had a great need: '*J'ai envie de faire pipi, Monsieur.*' At last somebody who could speak French amidst the whole bevy of health officials and personalities who had come out for these 'poor little crash victims'.

Locals brought food – chocolate and oranges – into the Sheepbank House. It was the first food that some of the girls had eaten in nearly twenty-four hours. Oonagh Guinness, Madame Rivière and the nurses and doctors ministered to everybody like angels.

When Pat O'Brien got down onto the road, he could see the light from the fire by the house about half a mile away. With the girl on his shoulders, supported by Criostoir Byrne, he dragged one weary foot after another, eventually collapsing inside the Sheepbank House. 'I wasn't able to go up [the mountain] any more. I was fatigued and Lady Oranmore said, "We'll give these men a cup of tea," which was lovely.'

The ambulances were now congregating at the foot of the mountain near the Sheepbank House. Pat O'Brien, with the girl on his shoulders, then made for the first ambulance on the road, only to find it locked and empty. 'The driver had gone up the mountain, which he shouldn't have done – Sergeant McNally was furious. But there were three or four other ambulances and I helped to put her in one.' He noticed she had a medallion on her neck with the name Jacqueline inscribed on it. 'I left then. I was saturated but still had to walk all the way home.'

Twenty-six

'There are twenty-six people in Ireland today who can thank their lucky stars that they are still alive,' reported *The Irish Times*. 'Anybody who examined the scene in the clear light of day found it difficult to imagine how anybody could have survived.'

Before going out to cut turf on the bog, Pat O'Brien went back to look at the wreck of the plane in the early morning. Restored to his full strength by a breakfast of rashers, egg and toast, he cycled the five miles to the Sally Gap Road. Propping his bicycle against a rock on the roadside overlooking Lough Tay, he retraced his steps from the night before, following the Piper's Brook up the side of Djouce Mountain. As he climbed to the top of the mountain, a gentle breeze was blowing and the sun rose over a calm Irish Sea. The sun broke over the mountains, bathing the scene in a freshness that seemed inappropriate to what it exposed. It was like the dawn of peace over a 'war-devastated land' as one of the papers reported.

Looking out to the east, waves broke on the sea beyond the Sugarloaf and the Calary Bog. Skerries and Howth Head stood out. The Welsh Hills were quite clear, as were the

Mountains of Mourne, eighty miles away. He climbed higher. To the north of the mountain, he could see the empty Glensoulan Valley, which separated Djouce from Maulin and Tonduff, and where the River Dargle flowed before tumbling into the Deerpark at the Watergates. It was here, sixteen hours earlier, that Chantal, Andrée and Capitaine Habez had come dangerously close to falling over Ireland's highest waterfall after wandering in the storm for four hours in search of help. War Hill, close by, sat in front of Tonduff and the furrowed brow of Kippure.

Turning to the south, the Table Mountain and the smaller domes leading to Lugnaquilla were in sharp profile. A kestrel hovered over Lough Tay, where the Fancy Rock was reflected in the water. The rock cast a shadow over the lodge of Luggala.

Westwards, the peaks of the mountains he knew so well – Gravale, Duff Hill, Tonelagee and Mullaghcleevaun – formed a dark-blue backdrop to the wreck of the plane, which sat squarely on the boggy ground, looking as if it had landed by design in this remote corner of Wicklow.

A glorious vegetal smell, produced by the sun, was starting to rise from the bog. It seemed like a magic place.

Later that day, a stream of sightseers, adults and children, climbed the mountain from all directions to catch a glimpse of the strange sight; little boys ran over the hill making the sound of aeroplanes with their arms outstretched.

Sixteen-year-old Dermot James was one of the many Boy Scouts to scramble up to the spot. A week later he returned to take a photograph with his old Brownie camera. Hilary Hamilton, who had heard the plane flying low in the Cloghoge River valley, hiked up to the crash site with her friends Sam and Florrie French. She took some pictures with her Kodak Brownie. In one, her baby son Richard is pictured at the door of the plane with the two women on either side.

Several of The Irish Girl Guides visited the site, and Phil Crowley from the Catholic Girl Guides of Ireland brought a group of girls. Even Taoiseach Eamon de Valera visited the wreck of the machine. Quidnunc of *The Irish Times*, the writer Patrick Campbell, took a particular interest in the story. He noted in his 'Irishman's Diary' column of 14 August that, by sheer coincidence, he had bumped into medical student Bill Deely on his way to the plane. 'I noticed that the whites of his eyes were bright red after his sleepless night in the storm.' Quidnunc continued:

> From the foot of Djouce on the seaward side, I could see something glittering in the sun, up near the summit. There were tiny figures walking around this glittering thing. Occasionally, they disappeared over the brow of the hill. This was the resting place of the plane.

It took Quidnunc an hour to climb the mountain:

> a path led all the way up, a sheep track. By the edges of this track lay heaps of withered bracken, like seaweed marking high water, showing what a torrent must have poured down here on the previous night. And then suddenly, there was this broad, beaten path within thirty feet of the top of the hill – a foot deep in places, littered with torn scraps of aluminium, electrical cables, the two massive tyres. This broad, beaten path led over the top of the hill, promising – something – on the other side.
>
> I climbed to the top of the hill, and there a few yards away on the lower slope, against a background of distant blue peaks and steep green valleys, sat the Junkers 88 [*sic*], almost daintily, her tail high in the air ... She sat there quite square on the ground, at first sight almost undamaged, neat and tidy, alone here on the top of the mountain.
>
> But down to where she sat on the hillside led this same broad, beaten track, jagged with debris. She had gone through a wire fence, cutting the wire, bending one of the iron posts and entirely obliterating another.

As various officials, journalists and locals returned to the brow of Djouce, it became even more apparent that the passengers on the plane had had an amazing escape from death. According to Quidnunc:

> The most extraordinary thing was how the plane had not simply disintegrated when it hit the mountain. The pilot must have seen the ground seconds before hitting it and pulled the aeroplane up just enough to slide onto the rough ground at a very small angle and so the undercarriage absorbed most of the shock. This action must have saved the aircraft from disintegration and the occupants from graver injuries.
>
> And there was no fire. Had there been very few of the passengers would have survived especially as the majority of them remained in a jumbled heap on the floor.

In modern terminology, what had happened to the aircraft is known as CFIT – Controlled Flight into Terrain. The term suggests that the crew had no sense they were about to crash.

'I do not know of any place for many miles in that direction where there is such a raised platform covered by a cushion of heather and moss where the plane could have made a skid landing without being more badly damaged,' said Arthur Tomkins.

According to one expert, the pilot could have become disoriented while circling the Cloghoge Valley and driven his machine unwittingly into the dark waters of Lough Tay.

Quidnunc was one of the first journalists to examine the inside of the plane.

> I walked up close to her. She was rocking a little in the wind that came rushing down from the valley. In the cabin the first thing I saw was the splints – splints of every shape and size, some bound with cotton wadding. There was a French prayer book. There were several small navy-blue berets lying about, with tricolour linings. Stacked along one side of the cabin were tightly filled rucksacks. On top of the radio set

just aft of the cockpit was a large sodden piece of turf.

In the pilot's seat lay his helmet. The control-wheel was wrenched in half. The throttle levers were bent backward. One of the windows was splintered.

The intrepid Quidnunc walked back down the mountain and made his way to St Michael's Hospital, Dun Laoghaire, in the hope of interviewing some of the girls for *The Irish Times*. Thirteen of the girls had been admitted during the night. In St Michael's the house surgeon, Dr Donal Meagher, was one of the first to testify to the girls' wonderful spirit: 'They are the bravest people I have ever met. We're hopelessly over-crowded, there are so many of them, but they haven't made a single complaint.' He later told Quidnunc: 'Some of the girls are in considerable pain, but they are unbelievably bright and cheerful.'

'I am very proud of all my girls,' said the dark, good-looking pilot, sitting up in his hospital bed, bandage wrapped around his head.

Twenty-seven

Françoise Béchet felt someone touching her head. Her eyes were unfocused and she drifted, hopelessly confused. And then she heard a faraway voice saying, 'She's still got a bit of metal in her eyelid. Maybe I'll give it to her as a souvenir after the operation.' Later, she heard a priest saying, 'Mademoiselle, you are going to receive the last rites.'

But Françoise wasn't ready to die. Oh Saviour, she prayed, at eighteen years of age I love life. She hesitated ... But if that is what you want, then here I am. *Domine, tantum dic verbo, et sanabitur anima mea.*

Three days later, she awoke and saw three doctors leaning over her. 'I asked one of the doctors for the bit of metal from my eye.' In beds opposite her were two other Guides. She could hear them whispering, discussing the accident and talking about the *feux follets*.

She fell again into a reverie. She was back on the plane. 'We have arrived at the airport with one engine missing!' she cried. Then she seemed to be walking in mud.

'Poor Françoise,' the other Guides said. 'You haven't understood what has happened.'

After one week Françoise Béchet, with stitches in her right

eyelid, was eventually taken off the danger list. What became of the extracted piece of metal remains unexplained.

The injured girls and crew had been brought by ambulance to St Michael's, Dun Laoghaire, St Bricin's on the northside of Dublin or the Wicklow Hospital.

Michael Rooney of the St Kevin's Bus Company had helped to put some of them into the ambulances on the Sally Gap Road. When he found an ambulance with no driver, he got into the vehicle himself and drove three of the less injured girls to Keenan's Hotel in Roundwood before taking them to St Michael's Hospital.

Antoinette Nattier recalled: 'We arrived in a hotel. In the entrance hall there was a big mirror.' Catching a glimpse of her pitiful reflection, 'soaking wet hair, stuck down around our faces', she wondered for a moment what had happened to 'these valiant girls who were supposed to be representing France'.

'They're all speaking French!' said Betty Halpin's neighbour Ned Lennon. 'Put your uniform on quick Betty and get up to St Michael's straight away. It's pandemonium up there.' Betty Halpin, a Sea Ranger in Dun Laoghaire, had opened her front door to the local fireman Ned Lennon – exhausted from working all night on the mountain. The Dun Laoghaire fire brigade had been one of the first to arrive at the Mount Maulin Hotel to collect the casualties: Chantal, Andrée and the pilot. They had, therefore, worked longer and harder than any other crew.

Major General MacNeill of the army later paid tribute to their 'cheerfulness, discipline and efficiency' during the rescue operation. He added that it was a pleasure to be associated with such men. 'Dun Laoghaire may be very proud of them.'

Betty immediately changed into her navy-blue skirt and

knitted jumper, not forgetting to attach her white lanyard to her leather belt. She jumped onto her bicycle and pedalled as quickly as she could to the hospital. On her way into the ward, she passed some of the French girls' luggage, which was lining the corridor: torn rucksacks with peat still clinging to them.

She didn't speak a word of French but 'we had a way of communicating … as Guides. I spoke to a girl called Eliane Lemonnier.'

Chantal, Andrée and Capitaine Habez were the first arrivals at St Michael's Hospital, followed by Michel Tourret, the navigator, and the wireless operator, Daniel Duran.

It soon became apparent to those less injured – *les trois valides*, Chantal and Andrée – that they had come out of this episode remarkably unscathed. The French minister, Jean Rivière, stated:

> It was fortunate that the machine landed on soft boggy ground, or the casualties could have been dreadful.
>
> It was really an extraordinary piece of luck that we had not a greater disaster. The fact that the fuselage held together provided shelter for the girls during the twelve hours or more they had to wait until help arrived or they would have suffered very much from exposure, particularly those who were severely shocked.

'If the fuselage of the plane had smashed and the girls had been exposed to the torrential rains and the biting wind which tore across the mountain at that altitude, they must all have been dead from exposure before help reached them,' said Father Keohane, one of the priests from Glencree.

Initial examination of the girls in St Michael's indicated that, apart from Geneviève Bétrancourt, they had survived with relatively clean fractures. Agnès Laporte, Sylvia Ostrowetsky and Janine Alexandre all had what looked like broken collarbones. Odile Stahlberger had a pain down her right side and had probably broken a rib. Françoise Béchet and Ginette Martin had injuries to their eyes but were suffering mostly from shock. *Les trois valides* had only superficial bruising.

'I find myself in a hospital ward with two of the most seriously injured. I am able to help, as I am less seriously injured,' noted Janine.

Three of the crew – Christian Habez, Michel Tourret and Daniel Duran – had escaped with what looked like minor cuts and grazes. Capitaine Habez quickly scribbled a telegram to his girlfriend, Georgette Mathelin, at the Hotel Palais on the Quai Megisserie in Paris:

SAIN SAUF – SUIS HOPITAL DUBLIN BAISERS CHRISTIAN

Michel Tourret wrote one to his mother in Aix en Provence:

BONNES NOUVELLES DUBLIN. TENDRESSES TOURRET

Unlike Françoise, Odile Lecoquière realised straight away, on opening one eye that she was lying in a hospital bed. In the corridor outside, she could see a pile of blankets and the damaged rucksacks, soiled with mud. The next day she changed wards. She was bruised all over and her leg was sore. 'Are you still feeling pain?' asked the doctor in English. 'You've just got a deep cut in your left leg, a big knock on the head. Nothing broken. Your parents have received a telegram: "ODILE UNHARMED AFTER PLANE CRASH."' Odile blinked and smiled at the doctor. She didn't understand a word.

In St Bricin's military hospital on the north side of Dublin, Captain Laffan came on duty early on Tuesday morning. His diary of that day records:

> 13 August 1946. Found great commotion in Bricin's on arrival as seven French girls had been admitted there during the night after they were taken from a crashed plane in the Wicklow Hills – some of them severely injured. They were

all suffering from shock and hypothermia. Six were
operated on immediately.

One of these 'girls' was the air hostess, Antoinette de
Brimont. She had broken her finger and her jaw and had a
large cut across her face. She was only able to communicate
by nodding.

Jacqueline Conort, Micheline Bourdeauducq, Catherine
de Geuser and Nicole Jacques-Léon, it was confirmed by X-
ray, had all broken their legs. In addition, Catherine had a
broken collarbone. Magali Noyer appeared to have a
fractured skull. Antoinette Emo's ankle was broken and a
severed vein was 'bleeding freely'.

Ward One was one of six in St Bricin's. It was made
available so the six girls and air hostess could be together in
what was otherwise an entirely male hospital. During the war
St Bricin's had been a prime hospital for the army and thus
had received a considerable amount of extra money. This
enabled it to maintain a good laboratory, an X-ray department, surgeons and anaesthetists, operating tables and a liberal
supply of penicillin. There was no shortage of nurses to look
after the patients and when it was learnt that a group of
'pretty young French girls' had been admitted to the hospital,
there was no shortage of orderlies volunteering for duty.

The condition of the patients in St Bricin's was described
as serious: 'I am unable to state now whether some of these
patients may not die; they are all seriously ill. If they do not
die they will be fit for removal from here in twenty-one days'
time,' stated the commanding officer with military efficiency.

Georges Biagioni, the engineer, was brought to Wicklow
Hospital. Separated from Michel Tourret and Daniel Duran,
he had wandered on the mountain, shocked and disoriented,
for most of the night. He eventually collapsed and was
picked up early in the morning and brought to the hospital.

Anne Lemonnier was also brought to Wicklow Hospital.
She remained in a coma.

Saint Lô 1945

Vire will wind in other shadows
unborn through the bright ways tremble
and the old mind
ghost-abandoned
sink into its havoc

Samuel Beckett

Printed in *The Irish Times*, 24 June 1946

Twenty-eight

Jean Rivière despatched telegrams to the parents of the girls. 'But I want to tell you that the Minister to France and Madame Rivière were splendid,' Eileen Beatty later wrote to Madame de Beaulieu. Awarded the Légion d'honneur on 27 February that year, Monsieur Rivière had seen service in the First World War, part of a glowing diplomatic career that spanned more than twenty-five years.

The telegrams' wording was designed to inform but not alarm – it was all too close to the times, during the war, when a telegram was an ominous thing, a harbinger of bad news. It was only a matter of time before details of the crash were broadcast on the radio and appeared in the morning editions of the French newspapers.

With a broken collarbone and a 'wound' on her leg, Catherine de Geuser's condition was said not to be serious.

ACCIDENT AVIATION IRLANDE CATHERINE CLAVICULE
CASSEE ET BLESSURE JAMBE ETAT SANS GRAVITE

Many of the telegrams – sent 'On French Government Service' – included the wording *'bon état'*, belying the seriousness of some of the injuries. As it happened, the benign wording only served to worry some of the parents further. Other telegrams went astray.

Micheline's telegram gave no indication of how serious her condition was:

ACCIDENT AVIATION IRLANDE MICHELINE FRACTURE FEMUR DROIT HOSPITALISEE DUBLIN TRES BON ETAT

Jacqueline Conort's parents received the following:

ACCIDENT AVIATION IRLANDE JACQUELINE ENTORSE ETAT TRES SATISFAISANT

But they were not satisfied. That their daughter had been involved in a plane crash and escaped with only a sprained ankle sounded impossible. At best, they thought she was much more seriously injured and even feared she may have died.

In Le Havre, Odile Lecoquière's uncle worked for a Texan cotton merchant. Following his daily routine, he read the early morning papers before most people were up. Although some of the names were incorrect, he surmised from the newspaper headlines that one of the casualties, 'Odette Lequiere', was his niece. He decided to pay an impromptu visit to his sister, Odile's mother. Realising that news of the tragedy had not yet reached her, he declined to be the bearer of such worrying yet unspecific evidence. Madame Lecoquière only realised why he had turned up – *en passant* – when she received a telegram later stating that Odile was unharmed after a plane crash.

Janine's family in Saint Lô also heard of the crash before the telegram arrived.

> My brother and sister heard on the radio that a plane carrying French Girl Guides to Ireland had crashed. The plane had disappeared in the mountains in Ireland – nothing more was known. Luckily my mother didn't hear this information. My brother immediately went round to the Irish Hospital.

The Irish Hospital, built on a slope and commanding a pleasant view of the valley and the Vire River, had been officially inaugurated in April 1946. In August it was working to full capacity under the direction of Colonel McKinney, director of the army medical services. One of the hospital's more famous recruits was its storekeeper and interpreter, Samuel Beckett.

With 115 beds and a staff of 9 doctors, a matron and 30 nurses, it was the best-equipped hospital for miles. The people of Saint Lô were very grateful for the hospital, without which they would have found themselves in a very sorry state indeed.

Janine's brother rushed through the gateway of the hospital, past the long, low wooden buildings. According to Janine:

> The wheels were thus set in motion by the Irish medical team to obtain news from Dublin. This took place very quickly and when the official telegram arrived, saying that we had been found, my brother was able to give my mother reassuring details about the state of my health.

Once again the Irish Hospital in Saint Lô had come to the aid of the French. As Janine's brother left the grounds of the complex, the smell of Irish peat briquettes wafted from the hospital's kitchens, where two chefs, a Frenchman and a German prisoner of war, cooked together.

Madame de Beaulieu was also telegrammed with an update on the girls' conditions and was informed that, whilst Françoise Béchet and Agnès Laporte were out of danger, the surgeons were reserving their opinion on Anne Lemonnier and Geneviève Bétrancourt, both of whom were too shocked to be operated on immediately:

> CHIRURGIEN BONNE IMPRESSION BECHET LAPORTE STOP RESERVE OPINION SUR BETRANCOURT ET LEMONNIER ANNE TROP SHOCKEES POUR OPERATION IMMEDIATE

Monsieur and Madame Bétrancourt made immediate arrangements to travel to Ireland to be with their daughter.

Nicole's brother in Grenoble saw the telegram first. He ran up to wake his mother waving the piece of paper that read:

BLESSURE LEGERE GENOU TRES BON ETAT

'Nicole's a lucky girl,' he screamed. 'She's had the trip *and* the accident and isn't even hurt!' But Nicole was having difficulty keeping down anything. Two weeks later, her mother received a call from Ireland. The French Minister advised Madame Jacques-Léon to come to Dublin without delay.

For most of the parents, however, coming to see their daughters in hospital wasn't an option. Travel within France was difficult enough and travel abroad next to impossible. They relied on regular updates on their children's progress from the French Legation, International Commissioner Madame de Beaulieu and Mademoiselle Butte, the General Commissioner of the Eclaireuses. Most parents were satisfied with this arrangement and even reassured.

Monsieur Lemonnier put all his faith in the Irish medical teams. Even though Anne was gravely ill, lying in a coma in Wicklow Hospital, he was happy to receive news of Anne's continuing progress from the French Legation, whom he trusted to inform him of any deterioration in his daughter's condition. 'I am certain that Anne is receiving the best possible care and is surrounded by great affection,' he wrote, and went on to say, 'I defer to your better judgement.'

According to one letter received at the French Legation, Monsieur Bourdeauducq, father of Micheline, was not so reassured. He was said to be unhappy not only about his daughter's condition but also about the causes of the crash. '*Il fait mauvais esprit sur l'accident*,' wrote Mademoiselle Vercoustre, National Commissioner of the Guides de France to Monsieur Rivière. The letter went on to say that Monsieur

Bourdeauducq was anxious to see for himself what had happened to his daughter. He had decided to come to Dublin to conduct his own investigation and intended to interview all the Guides and Eclaireuses personally. The Minister to France was advised to treat him cordially.

Micheline later said she knew nothing of her father's disquiet. He had developed an interest in aircraft during the First World War and wanted to know what had happened to the Junkers plane but he did not travel to Ireland to see his daughter.

However Antoinette's parents were not happy that they had read about the crash in the newspapers before they received a telegram stating:

ANTOINETTE FRACTURE JAMBE PLATREE BON ETAT

Questions began to be raised about money and insurance, details of which were rather murky. With the prospect of Antoinette having to be operated on more than once, the cost of her treatment inevitably became a factor.

It was Monsieur Emo who, because he worked in the shipyards in Le Havre, managed to secure a place for himself on a cattle boat leaving for Ireland straight away.

Lilette's elderly grandmother was the first in the family to hear about the crash, when she turned on the early morning news on the radio in her bedroom in Saint Malo. Not long after, the newspapers confirmed what had happened. But the family received no telegram from Dublin. There was no Levy-Bruhl mentioned on the casualty lists of St Michael's, St Bricin's or Wicklow Hospital.

As her anxious parents waited for further news of the catastrophe, Lilette's father dispatched an urgent telegram to the French Legation in Dublin:

DONNEZ NOUVELLES MADEMOISELLE LEVY BRUHL BLESSEE
ACCIDENT AVIATION DOUZE AOUT A ENNISCORTHY

The message was sent at 10.45 A.M. on Tuesday 13 August. At eleven o'clock that same morning, a party of Red Cross workers from Bray found a girl lying on the side of the mountain.

Lilette had remained in the wrecked plane until the last girl had been taken down the mountain. She had assisted in lifting some of the worst injured onto stretchers and she saw how the stretcher-bearers looked at the ashen faces of Geneviève and Anne Lemonnier then looked at each other. It took at least fourteen hours to complete the rescue operation. It was more than twenty hours since she had eaten anything and her mouth was as dry as sandpaper.

During this time she remained cheerful and had already earned the admiration of the rescuers, who spoke of how she had calmly given comfort to the other girls, many of whom were in considerable pain, keeping their spirits up with her dry sense of humour and positive attitude. She 'moved among them, quietly, calmly and most efficiently', wrote the newspapers. They said she behaved more like one of the rescuers than the rescued. Lilette was reported as saying that she had tried to do what she could but 'inside the plane there was so little space, it was difficult to do anything'.

As the mauve light of dawn began to appear, she had left the plane in the company of a Miss Comerford and another local man. They soon became hopelessly lost and Miss Comerford struck out in a different direction to try to find help more quickly. She eventually reached a road and managed to hail a pony and trap to take her to Roundwood where another alarm was raised.

Lilette trudged on, her stomach empty.

Once the alarm had been raised, volunteers, including Pearce Kenny, and Red Cross search parties were once more dispatched to the area. Lilette was eventually found alone, her arm twisted, at mid-morning the next day. She had wandered about five miles in the direction of Glencree.

It was reported that she arrived at Roundwood Garda Station 'in good cheer ... none the worse for her ordeal and was able to sign the garda day book before being taken to St Michael's'.

Twenty-nine

As news of the calamity spread across Ireland and beyond, the newspapers talked of the 'girls' pluck'. Dominating the front pages of the Irish papers on 13 August, coverage of the accident took up as much space as that devoted to the Paris Peace Conference.

'DISASTER FEARS ON THE WICKLOW MOUNTAINS,' proclaimed the *Cork Examiner*'s first headlines, which in later editions read: 'TWENTY-TWO FRENCH GIRLS' AMAZING ESCAPE FROM DEATH'. Other headlines spoke of the 'DRAMA OF COUNTY WICKLOW MOUNTAIN SEARCH – MIDNIGHT CLIMAX TO HOURS OF ANXIETY' (*Irish Independent*); 'FRENCH GIRLS INJURED IN WICKLOW PLANE CRASH' (*The Irish Times*); 'FRENCH GIRLS' ORDEAL IN WICKLOW AIR CRASH' (*Irish Weekly Independent*); and 'DOLEFUL DISASTER' (*Wicklow People*).

What was reported often diverged sharply from what actually happened.

The French newspapers devoted less space but had dramatic headlines: 'ACCIDENT D'AVION ... SUR LA MONTAGNE ... AU SECOURS,' read *Dèpèche de Paris*; 'TRAGIQUE ACCIDENT D'AVIATION PRÈS DE DUBLIN,' was *Le Populaire*'s headline. Others were well off the mark: *L'Aube* reported that the plane had crashed in the Scottish Highlands. Chantal's former teacher read that twenty-three Guides had been drowned in a boat in the Irish Sea. Another report told of a group of Guides de France jumping out of a plane and parachuting over Ireland.

The *Irish Independent* reported how Paris had

> heaved a profound sigh of relief when it learned after hours of anxiety that there were no fatalities. Having regard to the nature of the landing and the mountain slope where the machine finally came to rest, the escape of the girls with apparently nothing more than some broken limbs, is regarded as extremely providential.

The popular newspapers concentrated on the personalities:

> WHEN OUR PLANE HIT THE MOUNTAIN: THE PILOT'S STORY – we ran into a storm when over the Irish Sea. Visibility over Éire was nil. We came lower to locate our position and then came the crash against the mountains. I was stunned; many of the girls lay around the badly damaged plane. It was agreed that I should go with two of the less injured girls for assistance. After hours of wandering we reached Mount Maulin Hotel. This is all I remember.

The articles listed the girls by name, often misspelled – Françoise Becket, Agnes de la Garte, Sylvie Ostroicki, Filet Levy Bruhl – and also the names of some of the rescuers. Pa Brennan's brother Anthony gave an interview to the *Irish Independent*, stating how he and two other boys from Round-wood were the 'first to arrive at the scene'. He described how they 'found a guard signalling with a torch beside the plane, the door of which had been wrenched off and a sack hung over it'. They went inside the plane: 'some of the girls appeared to be quite cheerful, talking excitedly amongst themselves'. The three boys carried three of the girls, who had slight leg injuries, on their backs down the mountain.

Monique recalled being brought down the mountain by 'this fine Irish man'. Many years later, Pa Brennan spoke of how good-looking his brother Anthony had been. He was always flirting with the girls – the wider the distance the less the harm. 'He was like quicksilver,' Pa remarked and 'struck up a little romance with one of the girls. They even corresponded for a while after she went back to France.'

The *Irish Press* reported:

> a fitful moon shone and the wind whipped blankets and wrappings but failed to drown the noise of the girls crying from pain, fatigue and loneliness more than 2,000 feet above sea-level.
>
> Nearly everyone cried in French or broken English for her mother. Curls in their hair were the sole reminder that eighteen hours earlier these children were spruced up for a holiday in Ireland.

Later some of those involved would feel a throb of irritation at the inaccuracies, the claims and counterclaims and resolved to bring them up at a later time. And as time went on the stories shifted and changed as they made their way across pubs and living-rooms throughout the area.

'When it was all over,' remarked Pa Brennan, 'there was some bitterness between the Enniskerry and the Roundwood crowd.'

Thirty

Ten miles from each other, and dominated by Djouce Mountain in between, the villages of Enniskerry and Round-wood reveal very different, if equally magnificent, landscapes.

The history and topography of a district is often reflected in its place name. Miles and miles of featureless, almost lunar landscape surround Roundwood, whose old name, An Tóchar, means 'the bog road or causeway'. Purple hollows and lonely moors stretch away to the mountains hiding some of the loveliest valleys in Ireland. There is a wild and rugged beauty in the vast extent of greyish peaks and heather slopes. Apart from the little piece of fertile earth round Luggala, the absence of tree cover presents an impressive, derelict mass, demanding some considerable respect.

On the north side of Djouce, Enniskerry, meaning 'the river of the rough crossing', takes its beauty from the thick canopy of woods that spreads across the valley, a mixture of scattered oak and beech shadows mingling with the rivers. Such density of green, with its ancient trees nestling under the mountains, is unusual in Wicklow. The trees also lend a deep and secretive air to the place – it was once the ancient stronghold of the O'Tooles but they had lost their lands long ago for refusing to submit to the English yoke.

The colonial hangover in this area came in the form of Lord Powerscourt but, as the diarist Claude Wall noted in the 1920s:

> Viscount Powerscourt is a credit to Ireland – the sort of man who should have possession of an Irish estate. He has beautified his property and done more to bring prosperity to the district than all the landlords put together. The best testimony to his popularity is that he came through the recent troubles in Ireland without receiving any injury and annoyance from any section whatsoever.

In 1943 Enniskerry, for a brief period, became a boom village when Laurence Olivier chose it for the Battle of Agincourt scene in his production of *Henry V*. The 510 footmen and 164 horsemen were recruited from LDF members and the unemployed.

With its mild, uniform temperature, provided by its sheltered position, Enniskerry and its surrounding townlands, Bahana and Ballinagee, stand out in contrast to the wild, exposed beauty of Roundwood and its own townlands, Ballinrush and Ballinastoe.

If you came from Enniskerry, one local said, 'you wouldn't ever go to Roundwood unless you had to', and vice versa.

In the *Dublin Evening Mail* on 26 August, the following letter appeared, its author identifying himself only as 'Give Every Man His Due':

> During the past ten days there have been numerous reports in the daily papers regarding the French Plane, which crashed on Douce Mountain on 12th inst. Most of these reports had a lot of incorrect points but there is only one, which I wish to bring to light.
>
> I refer to the praise given to the different search parties and ambulance units etc – which undoubtedly deserved

high praise. But one party who deserved great credit has not yet been mentioned, and that is the party of civilians and gardaí from Enniskerry who were the first search party to find the plane. This party was led by Norman Keegan, Bill Deely and Conor Hogan, who were the three first rescuers to reach the plane. They had been separated from the rest of the party, some of whom failed to make progress over the rough mountain and against dense fog and rain. These three men arrived at the scene of the crash at 10 P.M. and Keegan and Daly [*sic*] made the injured girls as comfortable as possible, while Hogan returned across the mountain to contact the remainder of the search party, and returned about an hour later with Sergeant Wickham, Enniskerry and Sergeant Kelly, Bray. Hogan and Keegan then descended the mountain and collected civilian helpers and doctors, and guided them to the plane.

I think the Enniskerry party deserve some credit. Had they not found the plane at 10 P.M. it would have been impossible to locate it when darkness fell fifteen minutes later accompanied by dense fog, which made visibility very difficult. The girls, most of who were badly injured might have been left to shelter and suffer in the wrecked plane until daylight.

The next party of rescuers did not arrive until midnight, having been attracted by fires lit near the plane as signals by Sergeant Wickham.

Previously, on 17 August, the *Irish Press* had printed another letter:

A Chara,

In your account of the rescue of victims of the aeroplane accident on Djouce Mountain on Monday last, it is regrettable that no tribute has been paid to the people who showed the greatest self-sacrifice and heroism, namely the boys from Roundwood.

The news of the crash reached the village of Roundwood at 9 P.M. By 9.30 P.M. a lorry loaded with local lads as well as three private cars was dashing to the rescue. On arrival at the Shepherd's Hut the rescuers from Roundwood, on the vague information at their disposal, impulsively rushed up the mountain, overcoming all obstacles of terrain, and located the plane. These boys, who had as yet no stretchers or torches, brought down on their backs the least injured of the victims returning over that almost impassable country twice and in some cases three times, to rescue the girls in the plane. Some idea of the nature of the terrain may be grasped when it is realised that the return journey from the hut to the plane (a distance of less than two miles) took over two hours.

It is only fair that public tribute should be paid to the wonderful endurance, strength and courage of those men of Roundwood, as well as to those who so generously supplied blankets, lamps, food and restoratives, without which the Shepherd's Hut could not have been 'miraculously' transformed into such a well-equipped First Aid Post.

Had the news of the crash been phoned to Roundwood immediately on receiving it in Enniskerry, the rescue of the entire party could have been accomplished by 2 A.M.

As it was, the Roundwood boys worked like Trojans from 9.30 P.M. to 6 A.M.

As an eyewitness, I can describe as completely incorrect, the statement that the French girls were hysterical. They behaved with magnificent calmness, courage and restraint, notwithstanding their injuries and the appalling ordeal of hunger, thirst, pain, cold and exposure through which they passed.

Beir buaidh agus beannacht
Is mise le meas.

Norman Keegan from Ballinagee countered with the following letter in the *Wicklow People*, published on 24 August.

With regard to your report in the last issue of the *Wicklow People* referring to the plane crash which occurred on Douce [*sic*] Mountain on the 12th inst. You made some statements that were very incorrect. First it said that the plane was found about midnight, whereas the plane was actually found at 10 P.M. Secondly, in another column, the search party from Roundwood got a lot of praise for arriving at the plane first, and for their gallantry. But it was a party from Enniskerry who arrived first at the place at 10 P.M. and the Roundwood party did not arrive until midnight. There are other incorrect reports, but I am not going to pass any remark about them. But I would like to see the people who were first at the plane getting the credit due, as it is the people not so deserving are getting all the praise. I am writing this letter on behalf of myself, Bill Deely and Conor Hogan who led the Enniskerry party, and arrived at the plane first. I am enclosing a report which is, and I can prove is, correct, and I would very much like you to make a correction in your next issue. After all, everybody has been thanked for the help, but the Enniskerry party, who deserve credit, have not been mentioned.

Hoping you will please correct your previous report.

Thirty-one

Some of the local men, Eliane Lemonnier recalled, who had struggled down the mountain with the least injured girls, turned up at the hospital the day after the rescue to collect their coats. There followed a steady flow of visitors to both hospitals.

One of the first at St Michael's was Eileen Beatty, who later travelled across Dublin city centre to St Bricin's. In 1946 Eileen Beatty was the Secretary of The Irish Girl Guides and, with Mrs Lillis, Area Commissioner for Dublin, had been responsible for organising the French visit. Today, in their headquarters in Pembroke Park, a photograph of Eileen Beatty, the third Chief Commissioner of The Irish Girl Guides, hangs in the room named after her next to photographs of her predecessors: a portrait of Lady Powerscourt, dressed in full regalia, the first Chief Commissioner, and her successor, also Lady Powerscourt. Eileen Beatty held the position from 1957.

Having spent an anxious night waiting for news of the crash victims in the Mount Maulin Hotel, Eileen Beatty later wrote about her own ordeal:

The long wait was the worst. At three in the morning we were told that the plane had not in fact been found. The ambulance men were then told to go to the first aid post at the shepherd's hut but when they attempted to do so, they found that the road was impassable. Luckily a motorcyclist passed by and pointed out that by taking a twenty odd kilometre detour, we would be able to get there by going round the mountain. This proved very difficult but we got there in the end.

By the time Eileen Beatty arrived at the Sheepbank House, only three of the girls were left to transport to hospital. She travelled to St Michael's in the last of the ambulances. She then made her way to St Bricin's Hospital.

Some of the dignitaries that graced the wards included Lady Powerscourt and members of the Guinness banking family. Monsieur and Madame Rivière and other staff in the French Legation visited regularly: 'The chauffeur came in with armfuls of food and fruit,' remembered Nicole.

Mrs Lillis and Ethel Moore, the International Comm-issioner of The Irish Girl Guides, went to the hospitals as often as they could. Margaret Hamilton-Reid and Estelle Moore, commander of the Rathfarnham camp, were able to converse in French with the girls. But the language didn't really matter: 'We were all "B.P." Guides,' said Mona Heary. 'Among ourselves Guiding has its own language for all nations; that is the only way I can explain how we understood each other.'

Bearing presents, Guides from several Irish Girl Guide companies made the journey: the 1st Bray, 2nd Wicklow, Greystones, Dun Laoghaire, St James, Clontarf, 6th Dublin, 1st Cadet, 21st South Dublin, 19th South Dublin and the Sea Rangers. For some, they had to admit, it was a very good excuse for skipping their Irish lessons. Muriel Berry and Gladys Finlay were two of the many Guides who visited the girls in St Bricin's. Muriel continued to correspond with

Jacqueline for some time afterwards. Phil Crowley, having visited the scene of the crash, now brought her group of Catholic Girl Guides of Ireland to St Bricin's:

> purely as an unofficial gesture of solidarity. They were guests in Ireland. We had no French – they had no English. And on both our visits, they already had French Boy Scouts to visit them ... I think they were more interested, naturally, in the boys than they were in us.

Magali had several visits from one couple in particular. This couple confided in the staff that she reminded them of their daughter, who had died of a serious illness the previous year. They wanted to give Magali a present and one day they asked her what would give her most pleasure. After a moment's hesitation, Magali asked for a pair of shoes.

> During the war, and indeed for a long time afterwards, it was impossible to get a decent pair of shoes in France. The ration coupon only permitted one pair a year. Even then the soles were made of inferior 'articulated wood'. [The Germans had requisitioned all the stocks of leather.] As a result, they quickly wore out and the nails stuck into your feet.

A few days later, a shop delivered three pairs of leather shoes, 'each more beautiful than the other'.

A stream of other gifts – illustrated papers from Limerick, magazines from Mullingar, books from Killarney, sweets, chocolates, cigarettes, cakes, oranges and tomatoes – poured into the big communal wards from well-wishers all over the country.

The girls were very grateful for these treats, not only because the hospital food was rather unpalatable to French tastes – 'Bovril and boiled chicken every day' – but also because these were luxuries they had been deprived of for five years during the war. It was 'fantastic' to have a juicy orange from Brazil – a fruit reserved only for festivals in France at that time – and the girls devoured them eagerly.

A 'wonderful smell of oranges' woke Magali in Ward One of St Bricin's. 'I had tears of joy in my eyes. This was the smell I associated with the Christmas presents given to children in my Protestant church.' It reminded her of the years before the war, before oranges disappeared from the shops. For many years after, she told people about the kindness of the Irish and how they had welcomed her with a symbolic 'Christmas tree'.

Fourteen-year-old Catherine de Geuser greeted her visitors in a cloud of cigarette smoke, a Players Navy Cut tipped in one hand, a chocolate in the other.

A photograph appeared in several papers of the pilot and navigator in hospital. With a cigarette clamped between his lips, Capitaine Habez proffers his packet to Aspirant Tourret, who is shown reaching out for a smoke. Beside him on the bedside table, a bottle of wine – French, of course.

As she sipped lemonade and puffed feverishly on a Sweet Afton cigarette, in short jerks, blowing the smoke out immediately and puffing again, Jacqueline Conort, broken nose and black circles round her eyes, wondered what her parents would think if they could see her now.

In St Michael's, Monique Ygouf sat up in bed in her green hospital gown with its quilted collar – *'c'était super-chic'* – and filled her mouth with cake and chocolate.

Thirty-two

Letters of sympathy flowed in to the French Legation. The Little Sisters of the Poor, the Brazilian Consul, representatives from TWA and the St John Ambulance personnel were only a few of the people who wrote. All testified to the girls' courage and fortitude. Letters in French arrived from members of the Cercle Français in Waterford, Irish Continental Shipping and other individuals.

In the middle of a heated exchange of letters concerning the banning of Frank O'Connor's English translation of the Irish poem 'The Midnight Court' on grounds of immorality, the following brief letter appeared in *The Irish Times* on 14 August 1946:

> Sir,
>
> As a friendly gesture of comfort to these young French Guides who have suffered in the crash on our mountains, I should be very glad if you would accept this £5.
>
> We so much regret the very unfriendly reception our climate has given them. I personally have such happy recollections of my own visits to France – amongst them one to Le Havre from where, I see, there are several victims – that I would like to show my sympathy.
>
> Maude Ball, Dublin.

The Irish Times forwarded the money order to the French Legation, the manager of the paper adding: 'May I too, express my sympathy with these young ladies, your nationals, together with the hope that they have by now fully recovered from their experience. I hope that on their next visit to Ireland the weather will not be so unkind.'

Bray Council stated that it regretted the accident, which it said was due to 'elements beyond its control'.

A letter arrived from France:

> My dear little sisters,
>
> This letter is to tell you how much your Chief Guides and all your sisters in France are thinking of you, after being devastated by your accident.
>
> A large number of us learnt about it during the Scout and Guide pilgrimage to Strasbourg. There were almost 5,000 of us and, as in Lourdes, we commended you to the Holy Virgin in saying, 'Saviour, those whom you love are ill.'
>
> Since then I have received many English [*sic*] newspapers giving details of the accident and I have been worried about the consequences of a day and night exposed to the storm.
>
> I wish you, my dear little sisters, a swift recovery and I kiss you affectionately,
>
> Marie-Thérèse de Kerraoul, the Guides de France.

In Dublin for a tournament, officials from the French boxing team visited the girls in St Michael's. They took away letters from the girls to deliver to their parents and families in France.

In her first postcard to her mother on 17 August, Janine wrote:

> Ma maman chérie,
>
> Dans un bon petit lit, je t'écris pour te dire que je vais très bien — choyée — bourée de chocolat, bonbons, oranges. Beaucoup de visites — aucun cafard — ma clavicule ce n'est rien — dans deux jours je serai debout. [In a lovely little bed, I am writing to tell you that I am very well. I am being spoilt, stuffed with chocolates,

sweets, oranges, lots of visits, no boredom, not fed up. My
collarbone: it's nothing. In one or two days I'll be up.]

The next day, one of the doctors walked up to Janine's
bed, seized her shoulders and, with a vigorous shake, pulled
on her collarbone, cracking it back into place.

Nicole wrote to her grandmother in Paris:

My dear Mimine,

I am writing to you quickly to reassure you. The journey
went well. My stomach held up. Blue sky, a sea of cloud, a
little bit of view. But an accident: fell in an air pocket over
Ireland. Hole in my knee, 15cm by 7cm and I've got a pain
in my heel. Perhaps broken foot. Glasses broken. Charming
welcome. Oranges, milk that I throw up. I throw up all the
time. Getting by in English more or less.

Kisses to everyone,
Nicole.

She wrote again on 21 August:

My little Mimine,

I am really well. There's no point in Maman coming – I'll
be the one who comes to get her. They took my plaster off
yesterday morning and I'm prancing around like a little
devil. The only thing is, it's bleeding and the bandage sticks
and pulls a bit. But apart from that my morale is very good
and has always been so. At the beginning I was crying out.
I have learnt not to yell any more and I have even taught my
neighbour [Micheline] not to scream.

There's a charming nurse who calls me 'Canary'. The
sergeant who is the *maître d'* is a funny old thing. We are
always under the impression that he has drunk too much
whiskey. The other day, Micheline was singing, so he told
her that she had drunk too much lemonade (for here we
drink nothing but lemonade) and he brought along two
empty bottles of whiskey and asked if she had emptied
them. She replied that it was *him*. He said, 'Yes' and he went
away staggering and swaying.

> Today they changed the plasters on those who had them. Micheline, who has a broken femur, has been put into plaster (again). The poor girl, she is in plaster up to her waist and half her other leg.
>
> I have written to Daniel [her brother] for his Saint's Day. I think that he will see that we are fine, spoilt and pampered. We've got as many oranges as we want – we've almost had enough of them; and chocolates, sweets, cakes and cigarettes. They [the other girls] smoke like chimneys but I don't dare to too much ...
>
> They have repaired my glasses. It's flat glass, not to my vision but it's fine nevertheless.
>
> Your barley sugars were delicious. As they came from France, I shared them amongst the other six [*sic*].

Five days later she was amazed, on opening her eyes, to see her mother leaning over her bed.

After the fall of France, Nicole's 'extraordinary' mother had protected her family in Grenoble at a time when Pétain decreed that every Jew was an enemy of the new Vichy state.

When the Germans occupied the whole of France in 1942, Nicole's mother, without any help (Nicole's father had died when she was five years old), organised their escape from Grenoble to the Cévennes village of Chambon sur Lignon in the Massif Central, in the heart of Vichy territory. Her brother Daniel travelled separately, narrowly escaping capture by the Germans as he jumped on a train at the last minute to join them.

Chambon sur Lignon, a beautiful village set three thousand feet above a river valley, had sheltered a Protestant population marked by repeated persecution and massacre by Catholic kings. So there was plenty of sympathy for the plight of the Jews. The village welcomed many Jewish children who had taken on false identities – although the Jacques-Léon family did not change its name.

Nicole, therefore, had no bad memories of this period, protected as she was by the villagers and her mother. In

Chambon sur Lignon they lived in a house called *Au Soleil,* where Madame Jacques-Léon looked after several other Jewish refugee children.

Nicole recalled how one day her mother took the children on a surprise picnic into the mountains. She later discovered that Madame Jacques-Léon had been warned of a plan to massacre the Jews that day. Oblivious to anything untoward, the children enjoyed their day out looking down on the village where *les résistants* only managed to thwart the Germans at the last minute.

Already operated on in St Bricin's, Nicole once again was oblivious to the danger she was in – the danger that had resulted in her mother's unexpected arrival at her bedside. Her coccyx was broken and she was lying on a rubber ring to protect it. A cage with a light bulb rested over her legs to protect her knee. But septicaemia had set in and her temperature had risen to a life-threatening 106 degrees.

Eight injections a day of penicillin and two of morphine failed to reduce the fever or heal the festering wound in her leg. She was beginning to think she would become an addict from all the drugs.

Despite this, Nicole was feeling more sorry for Magali and Micheline on either side of her in the ward. Magali's skull was fractured but she had insisted her mother not be alarmed – *Elle insiste pour que sa mère ne se dérange pas.* Micheline would often scream out in agony. Neither of her new friends was able to sit up. In the scheme of suffering, thought Nicole, she wasn't doing too badly.

Madame Jacques-Léon had been summoned to Dublin to sign the consent form giving the doctors permission to amputate Nicole's leg. The doctors and nurses suggested that one of the other girls in the ward – Jacqueline, Catherine, Micheline, Magali or Antoinette Emo – should warn Nicole what was about to happen, but as Madame Jacques-Léon's daughter was wheeled into the operating theatre, not one of the girls had the courage to say a word.

Four hours later the surgeon came out of the theatre to speak to Nicole's mother.

After four days in a coma, Anne Lemonnier woke up. One leg broken, every one of her ribs shattered and her collarbone cracked, she remained in Wicklow Hospital, too critical to be moved immediately.

All memory of the accident had been erased from her mind. She had no recollection of the flight, the storm, the crash or her transport to Wicklow Hospital. Casting her mind back as far as she could, the searching was useless: there was nothing to find.

The following day, 17 August, she was transferred, with the navigator Georges Biagioni, by the St John Ambulance to St Michael's Hospital.

The French minister sent a telegram on 19 August to Monsieur Lemmonier in Yvetot:

FRACTURE FEMUR REDUITE HIER JAMBE EN EXTENSION BON ETAT [YESTERDAY FRACTURED FEMUR REDUCED BY TRACTION IN GOOD HEALTH]

Reassured, her parents saw no reason to travel to see her.

On the other hand, Monsieur and Madame Bétrancourt hurried from France to be near their daughter. With multiple fractures in her legs, Geneviève drifted in and out of consciousness and kept seeing a sign marked Theatre. In an obscure way, she wondered what Irish play she was being taken to again in St Michael's. But the drama that was about to be performed would put her centre stage. Chantal held her hand as she was wheeled into the operating theatre for a fourth successive time. And for the fourth time the priest was there to administer the last rites.

Shortly before her parents arrived on a delayed flight from Paris, and as Anne Lemonnier regained consciousness, Geneviève slipped into a coma.

The medical staff urgently handed the anxious Monsieur and Madame Bétrancourt a form authorising the surgeons to amputate Geneviève's leg. Immediately faced with such an agonising decision, they declined to sign.

Weather Forecasts

EXTRACT FROM METEOROLOGICAL FORECAST ISSUED AT LE BOURGET, 7.30 GMT, 12 AUGUST 1946

Vent Prévu (en k.p.h.)	En Surface	En Altitude		
		à 1,000 m	à 2,000 m	à 3,000m
De Paris à Manche	Sud	SW 50	SW 60	SW 70
De Manche à Dublin	NE 10	SW100	SW 110/120	SW 120/150

METEOROLOGICAL CONDITIONS AT DUBLIN AIRPORT AT 12.00 GMT, 12 AUGUST 1946

Visibility: 3 miles
Cloud: 7/10 at 300 ft, 3/10 at 900 ft
Surface wind: 020°, 28 m.p.h. gusting to 40 m.p.h.
Weather: Continuous slight rain
Pressure at aerodrome surface: 990.7 mb
Estimated gradient wind at 680 m: 050°, 40 knots

Thirty-three

Immediately after the accident, two officers from the Armée de l'Air, Lieutenant Colonel Pélissier of the French Transport Command and Capitaine Fauré, his technical advisor, flew from Paris to Dublin to conduct an investigation into the causes of the crash on behalf of the French authorities. Accompanying them was the National Commissioner of the Guides de France, Mademoiselle Vercoustre, a qualified nurse who, the records reported, was accommodated in St Bricin's.

Although the aircraft was a military machine, it was transporting young civilians and, as a result, had provoked widespread publicity in Ireland.

In view of this interest, plus the fact that the aircraft had made use of the civil radio, meteorological and air-traffic-control facilities at Dublin Airport, Seán Lemass, Minister for Industry and Commerce, decided that the Irish authorities should assist the French by conducting their own preliminary investigation. The government appointed Richard O'Sullivan, Chief Aeronautical Officer of the Department of Industry and Commerce, to take charge of the operation.

Having at first failed, Richard O'Sullivan eventually

located the wreck of the plane the day after the crash. He realised that while he had been struggling on the wrong side of the mountain in the dark the night before, 'the rescue operation had been successfully completed on the other side'.

His initial examination suggested that the plane must have struck the south-west shoulder of Djouce Mountain while on a north-westerly course. He found the landing wheels, the centre engine and the mass balance weights from each of the ailerons and judged that the first point of impact must have been about forty feet below the summit of a ridge. The plane had evidently hit this part of the mountain with considerable force. Indeed, had it hit this ridge thirty feet lower, where the mountain dropped steeply away, it would most certainly have been completely destroyed. Richard O'Sullivan deduced that the plane bounced to the top of the ridge and then slid on the bottom of the fuselage for about a hundred yards, shedding the two outboard engines and turning round to the right in the process. The left side of the cabin was extensively damaged in the final impact.

On examining the cockpit instruments, he noted that the compass course showed 340 degrees at the time of the crash. It was also clear that the plane had struck the hill while in a climbing attitude and apparently at normal cruising speed. The 'sturdy Junkers construction had withstood the impact very well', wrote Mr O'Sullivan. 'It was relatively intact.' He found a briefcase containing navigational maps and another map of the Irish Sea area on the floor – 'obviously the last map to be used by the navigator'. The navigator's logbook, however, was conspicuously missing.

Richard O'Sullivan made an air plot from the location of the crash and this 'clearly showed that he [the navigator] had made no allowance for the wind velocity, though this had been transmitted to him from the Dublin control office and duly acknowledged'.

The Irish aeronautical officer showed this air plot and the

transcript of the transmitted wind data to one of the French officers who

> threw his hands up in a typically Gallic gesture and cried, *'Erreur de navigation'* in a tone of firm conviction. With profuse thanks for our cooperation the two officers departed at high speed in the direction of Dun Laoghaire, and it was clear that things didn't look too good for the future professional prospects of the unfortunate NCO *navigateur!*

Unfortunately, or fortunately, for Michel Tourret, he was too ill to be interviewed by the French investigators and avoided the immediate castigation of his superiors.

The statement made earlier by the farm labourer Leo Ryan, working in Dr Collis' outhouse near Newtown Mount Kennedy, was considered but afterwards dismissed by the investigators for the rather implausible reason that it must have been referring to another plane, which by 'coincidence was also in the vicinity'.

Aeronautical Code Signals (the Q Code)

QAM   What is the latest available meteorological observation for [Dublin]?

QAN   What is the surface wind direction and speed at [Dublin]?

QDM   Will you indicate the MAGNETIC heading for me to steer towards you with no wind?

QDR   What is my MAGNETIC bearing from you [Dublin]?

QTE   What is my TRUE bearing from you?

Statement by Capitaine-Pilote C. Habez
15 August 1946

Near the coast of Wales our compass course was 297°. A Gee fix was obtained approximately six miles before the coast was reached. We changed course 3° to starboard, compass course 300°. We altered our height to 680 metres. We could see the sea at times through the clouds. We remained at this height. At 11.35 GMT, as far as I can remember, we received a QDM from Dublin of 325°. This gave a QTE of 132° corrected to 10° to starboard, compass course 310°. We heard planes working Dublin so we could not communicate for some time. At 12.17 GMT, as far as I can remember, we obtained a QDM of 334°, which gave a QTE of 141°, which was 11° south of the track, so in forty minutes we have a variation of QDM of 9°. We then corrected 30° to starboard. Compass course was 340°, at 12.20 GMT, as far as I can remember. The crash occurred five minutes afterwards. We were just about to ask for a series of QDMs when the crash occurred. At 12.00 GMT we were taking the Met. Report from Dublin. Our airspeed during the flight was approximately 105 KTS.

The French army authorities spent the entire Thursday after the crash on Djouce examining the wreck and taking measurements. Some parts of the wing were found almost half a mile away. After removing some pieces of the aircraft – the wireless transmitting apparatus, technical instruments, a portion of the rudder and the control board – they left the remainder of the plane behind, telling the Bray gardaí that they were finished and had no further interest in it. Later that evening, officers from Bray Garda Station went back to the scene. They cut open the plane's six petrol tanks and destroyed the fuel, thus preventing possible accidents or explosions. With the prospect of an influx of sightseers, they were anxious to render the wreckage 'harmless and of no value' before the weekend.

As soon as garda protection was withdrawn at 9 P.M. on

Friday 16 August, local souvenir hunters and scrap men trudged up the mountain and started picking over parts of the wreckage. Some cut their hands in the process. Whole sections were taken away. It was said that gardens all over County Wicklow were littered with pieces of the metal machine. Parts were used to patch up holes in barn roofs and for garden walls. People made ladders from salvaged bits and hung their pictures by pieces of wire from the cockpit. Charlie Keegan admitted to taking a piece of yellow electrical cable about three yards long, 'as thick as your finger'. Another sideline was the manufacture of rings from the metal.

Employees from the Roundwood Inn went up with a horse and cart. They loaded one of the big BMW engines onto their cart. The engine sat in the car-park of the hotel for many years afterwards. One local took his horse up the mountain and pulled down a wing of the plane, which he later kept in his garden in Ballinastoe.

Richard Hamilton's grandparents acquired one of the tiny seats and two petrol engines – 'about three or four metres long and one metre in diameter' according to Richard – which his grandfather refashioned into speedboats with outboard motors attached. They stayed afloat for some time before they sprang a series of leaks and sank to the bottom of Lough Dan.

Propped against the wall of a garage was a bent propeller. In Ballinastoe, an entire hen house was constructed from salvaged parts that had been scattered for a hundred yards round the plane. The parts became the medium by which folk memory survives to this day.

Too heavy to lift on its own, a support for the landing gear was pushed under a rock, hidden away, to be carried down the mountain at some future date.

Some of the Guides at the Rathfarnham Camp, 1946

IRISH (CONSISTING OF THREE GROUPS: LEINSTER, MUNSTER AND CONNAUGHT)
Anne Jones, Dorothy Jolley, Anne Wood, Olive and Vera Sutton, Betty Moylan, Myra Healey, Mona Heary, Doreen Bradbury (attended certain sessions), Esther Blackburn, Vida Kay, Violet Manning, Alison Nugent, Anne Fryer, Poppy Clark, Hazel Allshire, Jean Goulding, Gay Langrell, Peggy Jewell, Elaine Wright, Joan Smith, Eleanor Benson, Ineke Mekking, Margaret Hamilton-Reid.
Moira Cooke (Group Commandant)
Helen Moore (Group Commandant)
Estelle Moore (Group Commandant)
Ethel Moore (International Commissioner)
Doris Findlater (Quartermaster)
Irene Richardson (Quartermaster)
Pat Johnson (Doctor)

DUTCH
Bep de Beer, Sonia Wijnberg, Anneke Fabius, Lies Kann, Hetty den Hertzog, Jotie Geerling, Jos de Leeuw, Riekje Kuus.
Johanna Redeke (Leader)
R. Boonstra (Leader)
M. Uilenriff (Leader)

Thirty-four

The accident met with by the French girls had now scuppered half of The Irish Girl Guides' plans. In their headquarters in 28 Frederick Street, Eileen Beatty, Mrs Lillis and International Commissioner Ethel Moore debated whether they should abandon their plans completely or soldier on. The consensus was that rather than cancel the camp in Rathfarnham, where the Irish Girl Guides had already settled in, they should now concentrate all their efforts on giving the Dutch Guides the holiday of their lives.

The Dutch contingent – twenty-three Guides in all – had already left Holland by boat and train and were in London when they heard about the French plane crash. Obviously it was a great shock to them but, after several calls from the headquarters of the UK Girl Guides, they decided to continue the journey to Dublin. On the Thursday morning after the crash, the SS *Longford* docked at the North Wall, where the ever-reliable Margaret Hamilton-Reid was waiting to meet the Guides in brilliant sunshine.

The Dutch Guides were said to have 'whooped for joy'

when they stepped off the boat and hopped on the bus for Rathfarnham.

The Holland they had left behind was rapidly returning to normal but it still retained many of the scars of war. Like the French, the Dutch girls chosen for the trip were from the most badly affected areas, such as The Hague, Rotterdam and Arnhem. Olive Sutton was later to visit Rotterdam after the camp and witnessed how its

> whole heart had been levelled. The only sign that there had once been a densely populated city was the remnants of foot-paths and occasional foundations of buildings. Everything else had been tidied up and swept clean. Bricks were piled neatly. There was no debris about, nor weeds growing high between ruined walls such as I had seen in London.

In some ways the Dutch had suffered even more than the French during the war. One of the girls came from Putten, a small village, where almost the entire male adult population had been put to death. During the night of 30 September 1944, a resistance group had shot at a parked German army truck. As a reprisal, the Germans burned a hundred houses to the ground. Later they rounded up six hundred men between the ages of eighteen and fifty years.

The men were hauled out of their homes and then locked in a small church and held there until trucks arrived to take them away to labour and concentration camps in Germany and Poland. Of the 600 who were taken away, 552 did not come back.

The Commissioner in charge of the girls was imprisoned herself by the Germans for continuing Guiding activities in Holland during the war. On her release, she was dismissed from her post as a schoolteacher and later worked with the underground movement.

Olive Sutton recalled how her two Dutch friends had suffered in different ways.

Lies Kann had lost both her parents because her family was
Jewish. The children had first been evacuated to live with
their grandmother in the country and, when the parents did
not return, they remained with her. My other Dutch friend,
Anneke Fabius, had lived on the island of Walcheren during
the war. To prevent the Germans setting up flying bomb
bases there, the British bombed the dykes, flooding it.
Luckily the city of Middelburg was on higher ground and
the townspeople were safe but cut off from supplies of all
kinds from outside.

When the Irish Girl Guides learnt from Ethel Moore that
the French would not be coming, it was natural, said Olive
Sutton, 'that we should be thrown much more together with
the Dutch girls. We soon found them to be good fun and very
interesting.'

> When our visitors from Holland arrived, they were accom-
> modated in the college dormitories, probably because they
> had come by boat and train and it would have been a lot of
> trouble to bring camping equipment and sleeping bags with
> them on their long and uncomfortable journey. We went to
> see them off at the end of the camp and were horrified at
> the conditions in the steerage cabins of the Liverpool boat.
> At least the dormitories were more comfortable than the
> tents, especially when the weather was wet.

Altogether, there were seventy at the camp. This included
the Quartermaster, Doris Findlater, in charge of the cooking
– 'one of the most popular people there', reported the *Dublin
Evening Mail*. A typical lunch consisted of large helpings of
boiled meat, potatoes, peas and turnips. One of the Dutch
girls, however, 'handed back her plate saying she was veg-
etarian'. Olive Sutton recalled that, generally:

> they were grateful eaters – not turning up their noses at
> things we might not have specially liked ourselves, though

on the whole the food was good and we enjoyed gathering wood and cooking it. I don't recall that any of the Dutch Guides did the cooking with us but they probably helped in other ways and we all ate together.

The Irish Guides admired the Dutch girls' suntans and swimming prowess in the freezing water of the college swimming-pool, fed as it was straight from the mountain springs. Olive said:

> We were a bit shocked by their lack of modesty when one of our lot reported they were running in and out of the showers in the college without bothering to wrap themselves in anything at all – it seemed the Dutch were much less inhibited than we were.
>
> Campfire evenings were wonderful, though. We discovered they were excellent singers and knew some of the Guide songs we knew but had also a large repertoire of songs we had never heard. We made camp furniture, lashing branches together to make tables and chairs. We made some expeditions out of camp as well and visited the zoo on one occasion, something we might not normally have done at a Guide camp just for ourselves.

They also made regular visits to see the French girls in hospital. Olive Sutton remembered in particular 'Ginette Martin from Nantes'.

Flying over the camp was the World Flag – the international flag of the Guide Movement – with its golden trefoil on a blue background. Beside it fluttered the Irish tricolour and the Dutch national flag but no French tricolour was hoisted.

On 16 August, a Friday, Mrs Lillis and Eileen Beatty arrived at St Michael's with Mademoiselle Vercoustre, the National Commissioner of the Guides de France. They announced that *les trois valides* – Antoinette Nattier, Monique Ygouf and

Eliane Lemonnier – and Cheftaine Lilette Levy-Bruhl would be brought to the camp in Rathfarnham to meet the Dutch and Irish Guides.

The girls travelled by car to the camp and were able to see some of Dublin on the way. They attended a campfire on the little hill behind St Columba's and saw the Irish and Dutch Guides perform in their national dress.

The following day, Mademoiselle Vercoustre informed *les trois valides* that they would be returning to France.

'How are we going to travel?' asked Antoinette.

'By aeroplane.'

One by one, they refused.

'If you are not capable of facing this,' warned the Commissioner, 'I must ask you to unpick your badges. You are not worthy of being Guides.'

That was enough to convince the girls.

When, at the airport, a journalist asked them how they felt about going back to Paris by plane, Antoinette spoke for them all: 'We will be frightened but we will go.'

They were even less reassured when they saw that the plane that was going to transport them was another Junkers 52.

Flying back with the three girls were wireless operator Daniel Duran, Colonel Pélissier and Capitaine Fauré (the officers in charge of the inquiry) and Mademoiselle Vercoustre.

In the *Wicklow People*, the three girls' return to France was mentioned in between a reported miraculous cure at Knock and a story on the price of poultry.

A 'short-lived flutter of excitement' was reported at Collinstown when, while 'revving up', a flame was seen to shoot from the starboard engines of the aircraft. Officials at the airport were able to put it out but it caused 'some anxiety to members of the French colony in Dublin, many of whom were at the airport to see the girls off'.

Standing in the middle of the cabin, Antoinette spent almost the entire journey clutching the rail of the plane. As one of the officers tried to coax her into sitting down, she pointed out, referring to Lilette, that the only person who had not been injured at all on the flight coming over had been adopting this position.

'The co-pilot came out to see me and suggested that I come into the cockpit.' Refusing at first, Antoinette reluctantly accepted his offer. Soon after, she was sitting in the pilot's seat, looking at all the switches and gauges. 'The pilot let go of the controls and suddenly I was in charge.' This was more like it. 'I was flying the plane automatically. We were flying over the Isle of Wight. *C'était superbe!*'

The plane landed safely at Le Bourget, where the girls' parents were anxiously waiting.

'I was like the prodigal daughter,' said Monique. Her parents took her for a splendid lunch. Wearing her torn skirt and cape, she felt all eyes turn towards her when she walked into the well-heeled restaurant. 'I was suddenly the centre of attention. By the end of the meal, I had told my story to all the other astonished diners.'

Another visit was made to the camp at St Columba's College on visitor's day the following week. Chantal and Andrée were invited, with Monsieur and Madame Bétrancourt, Geneviève's parents. They watched Dutch and Irish dancing and, on this official visiting day, the Irish, Dutch *and* French flags were flying.

Lilette was transferred from St Michael's to St Bricin's after the outing to the Rathfarnham camp. Captain Laffan noted in his diary for that day: '16 August 1946: Admitted another French girl to Ward One. *This* one is an atheist.'

But there isn't an hour that doesn't have its births of sorrow as well as gladness, and tragedy was about to dampen the spirits at the camp in Rathfarnham.

One of the Dutch Guides, Hetty den Hertzog, became very ill with asthma and had to be admitted to hospital. She later died. Irish Guide Hazel Allshire was given the job of releasing the flags at the camp to half-mast. Olive Sutton recalled: 'It was, we heard later, not really unexpected, although her family had hoped that the trip and better food would have helped her, but she had been very frail even when she arrived.' In a group photograph, taken at the camp, she is seen standing in the front row on the far right-hand side, the smallest of the girls.

'The service in the local parish church was a sad occasion and the only one of its kind I've ever experienced. The little white coffin was not buried in Ireland but shipped back to the Netherlands.'

That same week, Chopin's 'Funeral March' was played throughout St Bricin's Hospital. During a training session at the military airfield in Baldonnel, a military plane had gone into an uncontrollable spin and exploded on impact in a nearby field. The pilot was killed instantly.

In Ward One, the girls listened in silence to the solemn music. For the first time since their accident, Jacqueline Conort felt tears come to her eyes. She couldn't say anything; her throat was blocked with sobs.

Thirty-five

It started with the blankets: three brown blankets and one white one, bearing the red markings of the Dargle and Bray Laundry, went missing. A small stretcher disappeared. The blankets belonged to Colliers of Bray. 'It is imperative that we get these blankets and the stretcher back as we cannot use our ambulances without them. We should be glad if you would kindly look into this matter for us,' wrote the manager to Monsieur Rivière.

They were only a few of the items that were never recovered after the accident. It was the beginning of a lengthy series of correspondence that arrived on the desk of the Minister to France at the French Legation.

Many of the girls' uniforms were unsalvageable. Lilette was kept in bed, not because she could not walk but because, after a night spent falling into bog holes in wild mountain terrain and lying in the mud, her uniform was completely destroyed. She was waiting in bed for some clothes to wear.

Moira Cooke and other Irish Guiders were given baskets of dirty, wet uniforms to wash.

Magali Noyer remembered the washed clothes coming back to the hospital in an impeccable condition two weeks after the crash. The girls were asked to identify their own belongings.

> Having retrieved my pullover, I was vainly looking for the new skirt that I had got special permission to purchase for the trip.
>
> The navy blue uniforms of the Guides de France were much more numerous. There were only a few of us who had brown uniforms. All the Eclaireuses had claimed theirs. I was the only one not to find mine. There was one tiny brown skirt left, ridiculously short, almost like a doll's outfit.
>
> When I examined it more closely, I had to admit that this pathetic bit of cloth was actually mine. It had shrunk by three-quarters. Such was the poor quality of post-war material.

Odile Lecoquière was invited to try and identify a few of the recovered rucksacks that were lined up along the corridor of St Michael's. They were so damaged and full of peat that very little of their contents was fit for use. Antoinette Emo recognised one of her socks, beginning to moulder.

What became of the rest of the girls' luggage remained a mystery, although rumours abounded among the local population. When Pat O'Brien returned to the site the day after the crash, it appeared that others were there before him. 'You'd be ashamed to say it but I saw two men with rucksacks, local lads, making their way down the mountain. I told the gardaí about it – there were no guards there at the time.' Years later, Sylvia remarked that she wasn't surprised that some of the rucksacks were taken. 'I was very left wing even then ... and I understood that they [the Irish] were very poor. I was never against them.'

Six of the girls' cameras went missing. Even though a succession of letters was sent by the Guides de France to the French Legation concerning their whereabouts – *Monsieur ... six appareils photographiques, qui se trouvaient dans les bagages des jeunes Guides de Frances victimes de l'accident, n'ont pas été retrouvés* – the girls did not retrieve them.

The correspondence then turned to the delicate question of finance. The first dispute broke out in St Bricin's.

The orderly officer, Captain Meenan, found himself in trouble for admitting the girls in the first place. Nobody could say on whose authority the decision was made. It appeared that it had not come from Command HQ as Captain Meenan had thought. However, under the circumstances 'the orderly officer had no option but to afford sanctuary and treatment to the casualties who were in danger of death and for whom no accommodation could be found in civilian hospitals'. The commanding officer for St Bricin's, Peter Fahy, continued:

> As to financial liability, I presume the French minister will be responsible for the maintenance of treatment of these patients …
>
> In conclusion, I beg to state that not only was there no intention to infringe any regulations in this case, but, that actually the action taken was one that under the circumstances would be actively endorsed by a higher authority.

It was only the beginning of a stormy exchange of correspondence over bureaucracy and money that would sour the proceedings. It rumbled on for many months.

The question of cost and who was going to pay for the girls' hospitalisation was always going to be a sticky issue. With several organisations involved – the Armée de l'Air, the Ministre des Affaires Etrangères, The French Legation, the Guides de France, the Eclaireuses and The Irish Girl Guides – nobody wanted to take responsibility. The whole trip had been arranged rather speedily – somebody knew somebody who knew somebody else in the Armée de l'Air. The insurance was only for a minimum amount of cover.

Letters passed back and forth between the Guides de France and the French Legation. For Madame de Beaulieu, now occupied in organising the World Conference of Girl Guides and Girl Scouts at Evian, the last thing she needed was this Irish problem.

It was agreed that the Armée de l'Air would settle the cost of the crew's hospitalisation and treatment and the Guides de France would cover that of the girls'. Madame de Beaulieu was anxious to keep the escalating hospital bills to a minimum.

The charge for the public ward in Dun Laoghaire was two-and-a-half guineas a week. The charge for an X-ray was two guineas. On top of this there were the specialist surgeons' bills and the cost of the use of ambulances. The St John Ambulance charged £2 2s 6d, to transport Anne Lemonnier from Wicklow Hospital to Dun Laoghaire.

In St Bricin's military hospital, they agreed that the cost would be the same as that adopted for 'interned members of the belligerent armed forces' during the war. A flat rate of fifteen shillings per day was imposed and an extra twelve shillings for each X-ray.

The hospitals, surgeons and ambulance personnel sent their bills on to the French Legation. The French Legation forwarded the bills to the Armée de l'Air and the Guides de France.

No payments were made.

Madame de Beaulieu left Paris for Evian on 18 August and handed over responsibility to Mademoiselle Butte, National Commissioner of the Eclaireuses. Mademoiselle Butte wrote to Lilette, the Cheftaine of the Eclaireuses, recommending that the girls be repatriated as soon as was physically possible. Apart from the most seriously injured – Magali, Micheline, Nicole, Anne Lemonnier, Geneviève and, surprisingly, Antoinette Emo – she informed Lilette that the girls would be brought back by plane, arranged by Colonel

Pélissier of the Armée de l'Air, as early as the first week of September.

Mademoiselle Butte added, 'It seems excessive that THREE Cheftaines should remain for six girls. One is sufficient. Please discuss this with your Guide comrades to see what is reasonable.'

Chantal, Lilette and Andrée talked over the matter. They agreed unequivocally that they would all stay on.

But the surgeons' bills remained unpaid. The doctors contacted The Irish Girl Guides. Mrs Lillis sent a personal cheque for £35 15s 0d. The total bill continued to rise. By October it had reached £550 17s 4d.

Eight weeks passed. The Minister to France, Monsieur Ostrorog – Monsieur Rivière having long since departed for the Netherlands – wrote to Madame de Beaulieu explaining that the Irish authorities had intervened again in an effort to obtain reimbursement for the girls' treatment. The Guides de France should pay their bill – now £559 – without delay.

There was another reason behind his impatience. 'Ireland is strategically important to us as a stopping off point for planes.' The matter required tact and perspicacity.

In a letter dated 19 December 1946 – when the snow began to fall over Paris, heralding in the 'great freeze' of 1947 – Monsieur Ostrorog also suggested, as a diplomatic gesture, that the Guides and Eclaireuses should send Christmas cards to some of the Irish Girl Guides, expressing their thanks for the hospitality they had received in Ireland.

The final letter in an increasingly exasperated tone was dated 26 March 1947 and addressed to Madame de Beaulieu:

> Madame,
>   The Irish authorities have once again intervened in a pressing manner to me to be reimbursed for the expenses that they have incurred following the accident in Wicklow,

the total of which was already sent to you four months ago.

To avoid a further embarrassing delay, I immediately telegraphed personally the Ministry of Foreign Affairs, the Air Ministry and the Ministry of Finance asking that they get in touch with you, in order that this question can be cleared up as soon as possible.

After seven years of trials, when France is endeavouring to reestablish foreign relations, it would be extremely regrettable to give the impression that we are insolvent and that the presence of French visitors is a source of expense for the country, which receives them.

It is in this spirit that I would be grateful if you could ensure without further delay, the settlement of these expenses, which are incumbent on your organisation.

Veuillez agréer, Madame, l'expression de mes respectueux hommages,
Le Ministre de France.

Whether the account was ever settled is not revealed in the archives. It was a year before the Marshall Plan was implemented. France had no currency reserves and a balance-of-payment deficit of ten billion francs. The Guides de France, like the country, was almost certainly broke.

Thirty-six

'So slowly time passed in sunny Dublin,' recorded Janine. Oblivious to all the behind-the-scene squabbles of the French and Irish authorities, the girls were agreeably pampered in the two hospitals: one under the command of the army; the other, the Sisters of Charity.

To begin with, the days passed easily for the less-injured girls. It was just a matter of waiting. It was a healthy thing to wait – it gave them a sense of anticipation.

Journalists regularly came to interview the survivors and they wanted to know how the little one was getting on. Sylvia, *la Benjamine*, was photographed with the doctor taking her pulse and smiling at the camera. Sylvia was photographed next to Dr Brennan – 'a nice old doctor' – judging a dog show at the St Michael's Fête: 'Here Sylvia offers Mrs H. Foy's prize-winning dog Borzoi some of her ice-cream.' She was the princess. She didn't even look thirteen. She was tiny, full of fun and confidence. Playing the clown around the ward, keeping up the spirits of the more seriously injured, distracting them with her jokes, her mimicry. She could also speak English. 'I wasn't shy. I was always laughing and joking. It's the tradition in the Jewish community – if you suffer you

must always smile ... I was playing the fool ... because
Geneviève and Anne were suffering so.' Sylvia didn't have to
worry about her frayed uniform any more because all their
uniforms had been ruined. She was an equal among equals.

Having found her skirt shrunk in the wash, Magali's three
pairs of shoes, the gift from one of her Irish visitors, took
pride of place on the floor by her bed.

> I can certainly say that I was thrilled with them, stroking
> them all the time, imagining the pleasure I would feel when
> I put them on after I was allowed out of bed.
> However, the Guider quickly reminded me of my duty as
> an Eclaireuse. I was representing France.
> 'You have to share.'
> I therefore had to give a pair each to two of my unfort-
> unate compatriots. I have to admit I did not hand them over
> with good grace.

Magali was, however, allowed to choose one pair of shoes for
herself.

Four days later the shop van turned up again at the
hospital. The driver had come back to pick up two of the
three pairs of shoes. '*Quelle déconvenue!*' The misunderstanding
proved even more devastating for Magali when, a few
moments later:

> the Guider made me hand over *my* pair of shoes to one of
> my injured companions who was from such a modest
> background that she would never have had a chance to own
> such a beautiful pair herself.
> I still think today that if this generous gesture had been
> proposed to me, I would probably have accepted. What I
> didn't like was being told to give away my shoes without any
> choice.

Deprived of such a 'wonderful treasure from Ireland' left a
deep mark on the sixteen-year-old girl from Paris.

Magali suffered in silence. Silence was the ideal to be
striven for. In St Bricin's the girls were constantly reminded

that the air hostess needed quiet. Although the 'sergeant was charming', Lilette recalled that some of the nurses 'were very hard on the children'.

The nuns in St Michael's were even stricter than in St Bricin's, with a reverence for the doctors that they expected their patients to adopt. 'Don't speak unless you are spoken to,' admonished Sister Tomasina. Rosary beads swinging, she cut a severe figure as she paced the ward and kept a sharp eye on her recalcitrant charges who, as their health and strength improved, were getting up to all sorts of harmless mischief. There were plenty of ways to have fun, especially if you had an orange or tomato to throw.

The nurses in St Michael's may have been stern but Dr Meagher was 'adorable.' He wasn't at all stuffy like the older doctors. He would tease and make the girls giggle. They shared many a lighthearted joke at the expense of the strict Sisters of Charity.

The nurse would caution the girls over some trifle; Dr Meagher, with a wink, would pretend to check his patients' charts, causing the girls to break out in giggles; the nurse would lose her temper; and the hospital lights shone on a picture on the wall of the Blessed Mary with her eyes raised towards heaven.

On his day off, Dr Meagher arranged to take Antoinette Emo and Odile Lecoquière out for a few hours. Strictly against regulations, they crept out of the hospital. Waiting for them two or three streets behind the building was Dr Meagher in his parked car. He took them on a jaunt along the coast. From Dalkey, they drove up the Vico Road to Killiney and Bray. Apparently unnoticed by the staff, they managed to slip back into the ward four hours later.

In St Michael's, the French crash victims came to be known as 'Dr Meagher's Girls'. Chantal, Anne Lemonnier, Antoinette Emo and Ginette Martin were smitten by the good-looking young medical officer. His kindness left a deep impression on them and their friendship continued for many years after their return to France.

Parcels of food and gifts continued to be delivered on a daily basis by well-wishers. A smell of oranges, bananas, cigarettes and stewed tea hung around the wards. The girls continued to receive regular visits and, said Lilette, 'I received several proposals of marriage.'

Lilette, who spoke English very well, assisted the doctors on their daily rounds by translating for them, even though 'the other nurses disapproved', she said. Watching how well the doctors performed their work reinforced Lilette's determination to take up medicine when she returned to France.

Lilette went shopping in Dublin to buy basic clothes for the girls: socks, sandals and shirts. On her way, she walked down Infirmary Road and passed big heaps of turf drying out in the Phoenix Park. She strolled down Henry Street and O'Connell Street and saw the street traders with impeccable white aprons, shouting their wares in hoarse, strained voices. Bananas, very green, were 1s 3d a pound. Oranges and grapefruit were on display in colourful piles. Fruits were available that she hadn't seen for seven years at home or could rarely afford to buy. In Paris, one grapefruit cost the equivalent of four days' pay for a skilled worker.

She gazed at the navy Derby Bowler in Clerys' window, priced 49s 11d. And she crossed over the River Liffey. There were queues everywhere, not all for cinemas and trams. The line of those seeking sailing tickets stretched all along Westmoreland Street. She wandered down Grafton Street and went into Switzers, where the ladies' hairdressing salon was advertising the 'machineless "Switzerwave"'. In Brown Thomas, she admired some linen sports blouses in bright colours.

Madame Jacques-Léon, Nicole's mother, also went

shopping in Brown Thomas. She dampened her finger, testing the quality of the linen blouses. She went into Macey's and Cassidy's on George's Street (now South Great George's Street) and fingered the jersey-cloth frocks in paisley and floral patterns. She debated buying a white lambs-wool jigger ('also available in skunk, opossum and musquash – astonishing value at nineteen guineas') but in the end settled on several pairs of woollen socks to take back to the family in France.

On her days off, Andrée Bonnet often visited the Dublin bookshops. In Europe and the Far East, a staggering two hundred million books had been destroyed or lost since 1939. Many libraries had been ruined or looted and scholars cut off from developments in their specialised fields. Andrée browsed through the Irish and English literature sections of Hodges Figgis and Eason's. Despite the puritanical censors (banned Irish writers at the time included Oliver St John Gogarty, Liam O'Flaherty and Norah Hoult), there were plenty of books to intrigue her.

Andrée was well enough to be discharged after eight days but the French Minister, mindful of her desire to learn English, found her a post as a governess to three children. The family lived in a country house near Wicklow and once a week they drove her into St Michael's to see the other survivors.

The doctors sent weekly reports of the girls' progress to the French Legation but it was Chantal – now staying at the French Legation – who made sure that the parents received these regular updates. 'Chantal was wonderful,' agreed Sylvia and Ginette. She spent the rest of her time in the hospital, comforting and keeping up the spirits of every one of the girls. She went to the hospital every day. There was no question of her returning to France before the last girl went home.

'The Cheftaines laboured efficiently to avoid any further

trauma,' said Janine. 'The atmosphere was joyful. The result was that the "holiday" in Ireland was transformed into a cushioned stay in a nice hospital.'

During this time, friendships were forged. In St Bricin's, Nicole, Magali and Micheline laughed and joked together. Catherine and Jacqueline from Le Havre became even friendlier.

In St Michael's, Janine found herself in the same ward as 'a little Jewess'.

> For me this was an interesting experience, because in my strict Catholic upbringing as well as in my family and in the region, I had practically never had the opportunity to know or meet anyone from a different religious persuasion. How I got to know this girl enchanted me, and I took her under my wing. Even though there was only one year's difference in our age, I felt much older.

'She was like a mother to me,' Sylvia said of Janine. Both girls went to the Lycée – the finest of the educational institutions – but their backgrounds were very different.

Sylvia told Janine about her parents, how they spoke in Yiddish and were poor and how this had made her feel different. She told her how her parents had originally fled from Poland and about the family's escape from Gentilly to the *zone libre* in 1942.

During the war, Sylvia's mother, a resourceful woman who had learned to live by her wits, had rescued a number of Jews from certain death. 'This *woman*, who was not able to read a book, saved twenty people.'

In 1942, a French gendarme had knocked on her mother's door in Gentilly – her father having already left for the south. When neighbours might inform on other neighbours, friends on friends, everyone was jumpy but the gendarme had an unspoken sympathy for Sylvia's mother and the plight of the Jews.

'Make sure you are not here tomorrow,' the gendarme warned, 'because if you are, you will be taken.'

Sylvia's mother quickly went to every Jew she knew in Paris and told them: '*Partez, partez.* The Germans will be here tomorrow.' It was in July, the day before the biggest round-up of Jews in Paris, which became known as La Grande Rafle.

A short time before the round-up, a small group departed from La Porte d'Italie for the *zone libre.* Sylvia's mother, the leader of this party, handed over money – 'you know the Jews always have a little bank of money' – to a *passeur* to help smuggle them over the border (the demarcation line) into the unoccupied southern zone of France.

When the party reached the border by train, they saw men in gabardine raincoats with dogs on leads: dogs trained to sniff out 'filthy Jews'.

'I have never been so frightened. We were in a train and they had come to take us,' said Sylvia.

And then a miracle happened.

Out of the blue, a big storm erupted: there was thunder; there was lightning. *Les chiens affolés s'étaient réfugiés sous les wagons* – the dogs darted under the carriages in fright and the policemen became preoccupied with the dogs. Sylvia, her mother and twenty others, including her little cousin – whose father had perished in Auschwitz – leapt from the train and ran. They ran for all they were worth over the border, to the relative safety of the *zone libre.*

'*Un miracle,*' said Sylvia's mother. The storm had saved them.

The image always haunted Sylvia's dreams. It made an impression that nothing would ever efface. 'All my life, I will remember this day, how I felt – it never leaves you.'

She talked about her time spent in a little village in the Corrèze *département,* south of the demarcation line, and her incomprehension when the villagers shouted, 'You killed Jesus.' Sylvia didn't understand who Jesus was. She told Janine that her brother and father had worked in the Resistance and how she herself had made the badges for the Maquisards.

Janine told Sylvia about her own family and her life at school with the nuns. She told her about the town of Saint Lô, about the Irish hospital and how grateful they were to receive penicillin from Ireland after the war in her 'capital of ruins'.

For Janine, life had not changed much at all during the occupation. There had been food rationing but, because of their good relations with *les paysans*, her family had been privileged compared to those in Paris and other large towns isolated from the countryside. She explained that, growing up in the protective environment of her family, the tragic events that subsequently hit her town intruded only superficially on her daily life. Ordinary life continued quite normally, as it would for any young person of her age. She got up, she went to school, she picked up good marks to please her parents and she had enough to eat. With her friends, she pursued inexpensive hobbies such as reading and listening to music on the record player. And, of course, central to this was the promotion of physical and moral health through Guiding. Although officially forbidden during the war, her company had continued to meet with discretion, never in uniform, in various private houses in the *département*. They never had any bother from the occupying forces.

The contrast to her new friend's life was startling. It was a rewarding friendship and many years later Janine was happy to be at Sylvia's seventieth birthday party.

And so August gave way to September. In the Irish countryside, farmers continued to be hampered by rain in their effort to save the harvest. Mr de Valera called for volunteers. Shopkeepers, professionals and civil servants abandoned their own business and rose to the occasion. Brian Hogan from the Mount Maulin Hotel recalled: 'We and our neighbours benefited from the help of the local forestry workers and we were very thankful for their assistance, especially as they were skilled in the use of the scythe.'

In St Michael's, apart from Geneviève and Anne, the girls were regaining their health, becoming stronger day by day.

Meanwhile, in her effort to limit the cost, Madame de Beaulieu was anxious that the girls should go back to France as soon as possible. She underwent some urgent discussions with Colonel Pélissier of the Armée de l'Air.

Thirty-seven

Diligently, Odile Lecoquière wrote to her parents every few days. Her patience had been exemplary. Her English was improving all the time. But as the dark greens of summer began to fade, the conscientious seventeen-year-old worried that she might miss her exams in France. If she failed to take an oral, she would probably have to redo the entire year of school.

The remaining girls were also beginning to feel restless. A slightly chill air seeped through the windows of St Michael's and crept through Ward One of St Bricin's: the first breath of autumn. However, when the girls breathed in, instead of the hospital air, their lungs filled with an entirely new atmosphere. It was redolent of ripened apples in a Normandy orchard; of the salt sea air in Le Havre, Avranches, Cherbourg and Nantes. It was the smell of the River Vire, the *bocage*, the alpine air of Grenoble and the bakeries of Paris.

Good news came to St Michael's. Odile and five of the other girls – Janine Alexandre, Françoise Béchet, Agnès Laporte, Odile Stahlberger and Sylvia Ostrowetsky – were to be flown back to France on Monday 9 September.

Surprisingly, the girls in St Bricin's – Lilette, Micheline,

Magali, Catherine, Jacqueline and Nicole – were also told they were going home. Only Antoinette Emo was to stay on.

The girls found it hard to explain. The patients in St Bricin's were still in plaster, unable to even use crutches, and yet Antoinette walked about unaided and in apparent good health. The Cheftaines, however, were not party to the delicate behind-the-scenes negotiations leading up to the girls' swift repatriation to France. When Monsieur Emo had arrived in Ireland to see his daughter, he said that, as far as he was concerned, she was not ready to travel. Commissaire Vercoustre had advised the French Legation and Madame de Beaulieu to treat him with circumspection and accede to his wishes.

On the day of the girls' departure, the faithful Quidnunc was at the airport to record the event, which was reported in *The Irish Times* on 11 September:

> There were four military ambulances in the car park at Collinstown Airport yesterday. In the ambulances, smoking cigarettes and gossiping cheerfully with their Irish army nurses, were five French Girl Guides, whose plane crashed upon Djouce some weeks ago. They were on their way home to France.
>
> Nearly all of them had broken legs or ankles. Beneath the blankets of their stretchers they wore heavy plaster casts.
>
> It was a horrible day. Rain lashed against the sides of the ambulances. The wind whistled about the airport building. From the apron in front of it came the roar of aeroplane engines, as Aer Lingus planes lumbered out into the mud of the field.
>
> The rain and the mud, and the roar of the engines must have created some unpleasant memories for the five French girls; but if they were nervous they did not show it.
>
> In the first ambulance was Jacqueline Conort, looking out of the window and smiling at the small crowd of

medical orderlies, drivers, army officers and Red Cross girls busy about their various tasks.

In the other ambulances were Micheline Bourdeauducq, Magali Noyer, Nicole Jacques-Léon and Catherine de Geuser.

Two or three French pilots and radiomen appeared, wearing their short-peaked caps, and a curious variety of overalls, blue trousers and waterproof battle-jackets. The door of one of the ambulances flew open and Antoinette de Brimont jumped out. She was the air hostess who had come over with the girls. She embraced the Frenchmen chattering excitedly. But it was difficult for Mademoiselle de Brimont to talk. She broke her jaw in the crash. It was bound tight with wire. [She had not been discharged from St Bricin's and was not travelling home that day.]

While the Girl Guides waited outside the airport building in their ambulances sixteen little French boys queued up with their baggage inside. They were some of the many French children who have been enjoying a holiday at Glencree. They too were on their way home.

Nearly all of them had a large brown-paper parcel looped about with string. One little boy had his luggage wrapped in a faded red towel. Another had a toy motorcar tied on top of a small, fibre suitcase. They were in a state of high excitement. Deafening yells ripped through the terminal building. The little boys chased one another around the pillars of the entrance hall, bumped into passengers coming off a bus, stopped and said most politely in English: 'Excuse me, I am very sorry.'

In the end, a French Red Cross girl, in that attractive sky-blue uniform with the sweeping, sky-blue beret, marshalled them into a long line. Then, carrying their extraordinary assortment of brown-paper parcels and cardboard boxes, they marched out to the plane that was to take them home.

The plane was a Junkers of precisely the same type that crashed with the Girl Guides on the shoulder of Djouce.

This plane was an obvious veteran. The sides of the fuselage were blackened with the engine exhaust. And on the door amidship, in neat, black letters, were the names of the countries that the plane had visited: 'Tripolitania, Great

Britain, Austria, Denmark, Belgium, Germany, Tunisia, Algeria, Morocco, Sudan, Senegal, Ivory Coast, Cyrenaica, Egypt, Eritrea, Abyssinia, Somaliland' and added faintly at the bottom of the list, 'Eire – Dublin'.

As the Junkers, with its load of small boys, moved off the apron onto the airfield the four ambulances, with the Girl Guides, came round the corner of the airport building, and lined up before the Douglas machine that was to take them home, in their turn.

The Douglas, still in greenish war-camouflage, was fitted up as a hospital plane. Webbing hung from ceiling to floor, with loops for the handles of the stretchers.

The first girl to be carried in was Jacqueline Conort. The medical orderlies first of all placed her with her feet facing the pilot's cabin. After some discussion they took her out again, and turned her round the other way. It was difficult to move in the narrow interior of the plane, but the orderlies were very gentle. When Jacqueline smiled at them, showing she was not frightened, they grinned back at her, rearranged her blankets, and asked if she was comfortable.

The others followed quickly. When the second ambulance backed up to the door of the plane there was a sudden burst of laughter from inside. When the orderlies opened the door we saw Micheline Bourdeauducq and her Irish army nurse in such a paroxysm of giggles that they were wiping their eyes with handkerchiefs. As Micheline was carried into the plane, and her stretcher was hoisted into its webbing, she was still laughing so much that everyone else started to laugh too.

There was quite a crowd around the door of the plane, in spite of the wind and the rain. As each empty stretcher was carried out the blankets blew around everywhere wrapping themselves about the heads of the orderlies. A pillow rolled over and over in the pools of water on the tarmac.

The Irish nurses in their green uniforms kept asking: 'May we just go in for a minute to say goodbye to them? We'll only be a minute.'

Six more Guides appeared, walking out from the airport building. They were the lightly injured ones, who seemed completely recovered.

Mademoiselle Rounet, the pretty hostess, stood at the door of the plane calling out the names. One by one the remaining Guides clambered in. Mademoiselle Rounet looked at her list. Everyone seemed accounted for. But then there was a wild, little cry from the crowd around the door — '*Et moi – et moi!*' A child of about seven [*sic*] pushed her way through. '*Alors*,' said Mademoiselle Rounet, 'Ostrowetsky!'

Ostrowetsky of the name far larger than herself, climbed into the Douglas, turned around and stood waving with considerable assurance to the crowd looking up at her. 'Goodbye,' said [Sylvia] Ostrowetsky, 'goodbye, and thank you.'

Then the door was slammed and we cleared away from the apron. The pilot, Capitaine Felton, revved up his engines, and the Douglas moved out on to the field. In another moment the plane was high above Collinstown, bound for Le Bourget. All those who had come to see her off sighed gently.

The take-off was safely over.

Soon after take-off, Janine remembered 'the terror we all felt when, almost immediately, the machine plunged into an air pocket — it appears that flying over the Irish Sea is a perilous business, given the frequent fog that covers it'. On the other hand, she had made a new little Eclaireuse friend (Sylvia) and was so preoccupied with reassuring her that she soon forgot her own fear.

Madame Jacques-Léon and Madame Bétrancourt also took this plane. Lying on a stretcher was Nicole, covered by a blanket.

When Nicole had been wheeled into the operating theatre in St Bricin's, she was the only person on Ward One oblivious to the fact that her leg was about to be amputated. The doctors had warned her mother that, because of the festering wound in her knee, her life was in danger and this was the only course of action open to them. It was, therefore, some surprise to her friends to see a grin on her face when she returned to the ward. What was even stranger was that the surgeon who performed the operation was laughing too, as he chatted to a relieved looking Madame Jacques-Léon.

Thanks to the excellent resources at St Bricin's Hospital, and the skill of the doctors, Nicole had emerged, after four hours of surgery, with both her legs intact. What the girls in Ward One had witnessed was the surgeon joking with Nicole's mother, saying, 'Madam, she will make a good dancer.'

On the flight back Nicole pondered whether she should sleep, as she had on the flight over or 'hang on'. She decided to hang on.

At Le Bourget Airport 'all the families were there, worried', said Janine, 'but very soon they were reassured and even laughing out loud, seeing us get out of the plane with our bundles – our rucksacks had not survived the shock.' Janine was also plumper. She had gained a few extra kilos from all the sweets and chocolate that she hadn't been able to resist in hospital.

Nicole's stretcher was put on the train to Grenoble through a window and she and her mother started their three-hundred-mile journey home. The doctor recommended that she expose her leg to the sun. It brought back memories of their house in the Massif Central, *Au Soleil*.

Nicole didn't return to school until 1 October, much to the envy of her brother Daniel. During her convalescence, a neighbour passed by one day and casually asked: 'Did you fall off a bicycle, *ma cherie?*'

'No, an aeroplane.'

The neighbour chuckled disbelievingly and went on her way.

Janine was reunited with her mother at Le Bourget. 'On our return to the station in Saint Lô, all my friends were on the platform waiting to give me a hero's welcome. Oddly, they gave me a gift of a collarbone of beef. I didn't really appreciate this but it was lovely to see everyone again.'

Before she left the airport, she said goodbye to her new little Jewish friend at Le Bourget Station, where the trains departed for the centre of Paris.

Le Bourget Station had been the main point of departure to Auschwitz after La Grande Rafle in 1942. The journey took three days and most died less than three months after reaching the camp. By the time the last train left for Auschwitz, on 17 August 1944, the eve of the liberation of Paris, 230,000 French had been deported for racial, political or resistance activities. Seventy-six thousand Jews left on the cattle wagons, amongst them Sylvia's uncle and several of Lilette and Nicole's relations – only one of Nicole's cousins came back. The majority of them passed through Drancy – a camp built on a 1930s unfinished housing estate near Le Bourget Airport. It became known as the waiting-room for Auschwitz. In August 1944 the last big departure from Drancy, in the summer heat, was one of the worst since the deportations began, resulting in many deaths before the wagons even reached Auschwitz.

Five days after Janine waved goodbye to Sylvia at Le Bourget station, the Nuremberg Trials began. One month later, Goering, the founder of the concentration camps, took poison a few hours before he was due to be executed for crimes against humanity.

Berlin Radio opened its broadcast that day with the hymn 'Life Begins Anew'.

The first of the crew to fly home was Adjutant Daniel Duran, the wireless operator, who had travelled back to France with *les trois valides* on 17 August. He was followed four days later by Aspirant Michel Tourret, the navigator, Georges Biagioni, the engineer, and Capitaine Christian Habez, the pilot. Capitaine Habez told reporters at the airport that, originally, he had not been looking forward to the trip to Ireland, as 'I did not know the country, but since I have come I am delighted to have met the people. Nobody could have been kinder or more attentive.'

The air hostess Antoinette de Brimont remained in St Bricin's Hospital for seventy days with her jaw wired together. She lived on a liquid diet of Bovril, milk, chicken jelly and soup. In the evening she was given sherry, brandy and a cup of tea before her mouth was washed out with bicarbonate of soda. She was discharged on 21 October.

Thirty-eight

Sandwiched between the news that troops were standing by in Bombay and the British government was in danger of serious breakdown, a joint statement was issued, on 23 August 1946, by the French and Irish governments, stating that the French plane accident had been due to 'an error in navigation aggravated by the unusual flight conditions prevailing at the time'.

The statement in *The Irish Times* merited five lines under the findings of a report into another plane crash near Shannon on 16 June, which took up several columns. On the same page was an announcement that the fate of twenty-one accused Nazi leaders would be heard in three weeks' time.

The French-plane-crash statement added that, following the joint inquiry, further action would be taken by the French military authorities.

The French official verdict drew on the findings of several experts in the Armée de l'Air. It was noted that the pilot and navigator had excellent records, the pilot himself having trained as a navigator in England.

The journey, the report concluded, had been executed as planned until the plane left the Gee system off the coast of

Wales. It stated that, as the pilot had not been warned of the movement of a depression over the Irish Sea, he had seen no reason to take special precautions. As a consequence, he was taken by surprise by the exceptional weather conditions, which had not been forecast when he left Le Bourget.

It was, however, noted that he had not made sufficient allowance for the drift of his aircraft, which the strong northerly wind was causing. As a consequence, he was flying well south of his track. (An expert has noted that Gee allowed the crew to control the drift of the plane caused by wind forces and so follow the optimum course up to the point where the Welsh coast was crossed. Thereafter their track tended to stray to port.)

Believing he was well clear of them, he had not taken measures to fly at a high enough altitude to avoid the mountains. Had he been warned earlier, it was deemed, he would have realised that he was flying far too low in the mountainous area of Wicklow. Four hundred feet higher and he would have cleared Djouce Mountain. Thirty feet lower and he would almost certainly have hit the sharp incline of the mountain and broken up completely.

If he could be reproached at all, it would be for not being cautious enough. He had lacked, the report stated, 'a necessary degree of prudence'. This over-confidence resulted in his not requesting enough information from the Dublin control office. Had he done so, he would have realised that he was well off his course.

However, given the unusual circumstances – and this was repeated three times – the sharp deterioration in the weather and the change in the direction of the wind, he could not be blamed one hundred per cent for not being high enough above 'an obstacle twenty-five kilometres from the airport' or for the fact that he had completely lost all sense of direction.

The meteorological office in Le Bourget was criticised for not forecasting accurately that a depression would be in the path of the aircraft over the Irish Sea. It was further noted that there was no point-to-point link between Dublin and Paris, whereby meteorological information from Dublin could be given to Paris for the purpose of amending forecasts. It was recommended that this be looked into as soon as possible. However, there was no official meteorological inquiry.

Neither was there an official technical inquiry.

Although the pilot, through his over-confidence, was guilty of serious professional misconduct, it was considered that the accident itself was sufficient punishment and a profitable lesson for the future. He was advised to exploit this experience on subsequent missions and in training those under his command. It was recommended that no action should be taken against Capitaine Habez.

The report also noted that the navigator, Aspirant Tourret, had not exercised tight enough control over the navigation of the aircraft in the difficult meteorological conditions prevailing.

Capitaine Habez and Aspirant Tourret were given a warning and grounded for thirty days.

The navigator's logbook was not recovered.

Thirty-nine

On 21 October, Geneviève Bétrancourt, Anne Lemonnier, Antoinette Emo and Chantal de Vitry were transported back to France on a hospital plane. Geneviève and Anne were lifted onto the plane on stretchers and Geneviève was immediately transferred to a hospital in Le Havre where she underwent a fifth operation on her legs. Thanks to the timely intervention of her parents and their refusal to sign the amputation authorisation form, the surgeons' solution to her condition had been averted. She was now on the road to recovery, although she was on crutches for a further six months. Many years later she wryly remarked: 'I spent three months in Ireland without putting my foot on the ground.'

Ginette Martin from Nantes was not on the plane, however. Although not badly injured physically, she appeared very traumatised and this had given the doctors cause for concern. A few days before the last girls went home, Ginette took the boat and the Golden Arrow train from London to Paris.

On one fine afternoon, three years earlier – many would never forget the blue sky, so much so that in years to come they couldn't help regarding a cloudless sky with foreboding – people were out and about in Nantes, walking in the park or shopping, when the familiar drone of aircraft was heard overhead. Nobody really gave it much thought, even when the sirens went off. They were used to the sound, used to the call to curfew. The Brittany town had been left relatively unscathed under the German occupation. Although the U-boat pens of Saint Nazaire nearby were always going to be a target for the Allies, the Martin family felt quite secure in their town with its port that was only big enough to be used as a repair shipyard for German craft. There had been sporadic bombardments and the odd incident, such as when two German planes had collided one day and fallen into Ginette's neighbour's garden. Otherwise the town had enjoyed a relative 'peace'. So when the sirens sounded nobody ran for cover.

At 4.02 P.M. bombs fell from the clear skies over Nantes. The object of the American attack: the port of Nantes. Instead, the inexperienced bombers (among them the actor Clark Gable) of the 8th Air Force Division released their lethal cargo over the Parc du Procé and in the centre of the town, killing many pedestrians. They returned on 23 September, bound for the shipyards again. They launched two attacks on the same day. By a similar error of judgement, the bombs fell on the centre of Nantes, devastating the same area as the first raid. Between 16 and 23 September, the town of Nantes was hailed with 1,500 bombs: 1,463 civilians were killed, 2,500 injured, 700 houses and buildings were completely destroyed and 3,000 rendered uninhabitable.

Leaving her two older brothers and father behind in Nantes after the bombings, Ginette and her mother had moved to the country with her two baby nephews. Her mother lived in a constant state of fear and anxiety for her husband and sons, who continued to work in the shipyards.

Some of the other Guides thought that she was too

nervous to travel by plane back to France after the accident, but Ginette later said that her mother had insisted she travel overland.

Two days before they left Dublin, Chantal and Antoinette Emo were invited to a huge rally of The Irish Girl Guides at the National Stadium on the South Circular Road. A Guide from every company in Ireland was present, as well as first-class Brownies. The rally was held in honour of the World Chief Guide, Lady Baden-Powell. Lady Powerscourt, the Chief Commissioner of The Irish Girl Guides, Mrs Lillis, Area Commissioner for Dublin, Margaret Hamilton-Reid and Eileen Beatty were there to receive their illustrious guest.

The day before, Lady B.P. had paid an unofficial visit to St Michael's to meet the remaining *rescapées*: Geneviève, Anne, Chantal and Antoinette. Antoinette recalled the frantic cleaning and tidying that had gone on prior to the visit. The girls entertained the Chief Guide of the world by singing French songs. Chantal remembered that Lady B.P. thoroughly enjoyed the songs, as they were some of her late husband's favourites.

During her address at the stadium, Lady B.P. spoke of how during the war the Guide movement had had to meet an 'acid test', but twenty years of peace-time building before this had made it strong enough to withstand the strain of war. 'In the occupied countries Guiding had helped to keep up morale.' Afterwards the Guide movement had flourished. 'In Holland, particularly, the expansion was noticeable. During the German occupation, 7,000 Guides had participated in the Resistance movement. Since the war, their numbers had increased to 40,000.' Her speech then moved on to France.

On the South Circular Road, as Lady B.P.'s speech came to an end, a hush descended on the crowded stadium. Heads turned away from Lady B.P. Some people stood up. All at once, everyone in the audience was clapping their hands and smiling at the two French survivors, *les rescapées*, at the back of the hall.

In her letter to Madame de Beaulieu shortly after the crash, Eileen Beatty had written: 'You can be very proud of your marvellous Guides. Praise for their extreme courage has been overwhelming. During their terrible ordeal everyone concurs as to their rare courage and calm.'

As the applause of the community of Irish Girl Guides rose to a crescendo, Chantal and Antoinette's hearts drummed.

Part 2

'I could tell you my adventures – beginning
from this morning,' said Alice a little timidly,
'but it's no use going back to yesterday, because
I was a different person then.'

Lewis Carroll

Forty

The Guides de France and Eclaireuses returned to their home towns: to the *villes martyres* – Le Havre, Avranches, Yvetot, Valognes, Cherbourg, Saint Lô and Nantes; to Grenoble; to Paris and its suburbs of Gentilly and Vincennes. Andrée went back to Issoire and the other Cheftaines, Chantal and Lilette, resumed their studies in Paris, the city of chestnut-lined avenues, where the leaves in the Tuileries were already tinged with gold.

For a short while, at least, despite the disapproval of some adults, they were treated like heroes at school and at Guide camps. They returned to their Guide companies and recounted their stories to other Guides and Brownies around the campfire. Once shy girls suddenly found they had developed confidence. The oddities of the event had altered them; they had matured very quickly.

The Le Havre girls enjoyed their brief moment of glory at school. In the oral exam she had been anxious not to miss, Odile Lecoquière told the story of the accident and her stay in Ireland. The more she talked, the better her English became. She ended up receiving a 'brilliant mark'. Geneviève found that she had plenty of stories to tell her friends in

Sainte Adresse: friends that she had waved goodbye to at Le Havre Station a lifetime ago.

Sylvia's father was very impressed with his little girl when she came home but her mother did not make much fuss of her. In Poland, girls married at thirteen or fourteen years and her mother was more concerned that Sylvia should find a husband soon. But one of Sylvia's teachers at the Lycée had told her that she would make a good teacher and writer. Later she would become a leading academic in the University of Picardie and publish a book about her father. *La Benjamine*, the daughter of the illiterate Polish immigrant, the victim and the rebel, was to succeed against terrible odds.

On her return to boarding-school in September, Janine was told by the nuns not to boast about the accident 'to make myself interesting'. Her adventure should not leave the walls of the school. This she found quite natural, 'as I did not suffer'.

Nicole's mother told her to pull herself together. And so she did, even though her school friends were fascinated by the wound in her knee – which for a while, she admitted, she 'milked for all it was worth'.

The very idea of coping on one's own would be unthinkable today. There would be an automatic assumption that every survivor was deeply traumatised and inevitably scarred. A plethora of experts – therapists, counsellors and social workers – would have been on hand to help the girls after such an ordeal. Indeed, the rescuers would also be considered victims and be offered emotional support. We live in an age of post-traumatic stress disorder, of syndromes, addictions and worries about self-esteem. These terms only flourished in the 1980s, although they did exist before then. Psychology and psychoanalysis were beginning to have more and more influence but at the time of the accident had not become part of how people defined themselves.

It was 1946, just after the Second World War. Children

were not encouraged to talk about themselves. Silence had been the key to survival during the war and silence was how they dealt with the trauma of the plane crash. They survived by putting it out of their minds. They were young and they were expected to pull themselves together and get on with life. They were Baden-Powell Girl Guides.

Nobody tried to sell her story to the press. Nobody tried to publicise her experience through a memoir. Nobody demanded compensation for her physical or psychological distress.

Nevertheless, the girls later said that they found it hard to put the event behind them.

Already damaged by her experiences during the war, Sylvia felt that the additional shock of the plane crash was 'too much for a little girl'.

Having spent over sixteen hours in the wrecked plane waiting to be rescued, Lilette said that she could not get the accident out of her mind for many years. But she never talked about it to her family.

For Anne Lemonnier, the memory had been sucked so deeply down that it would never be retrieved. Not only would she have no memory of the accident but also the memory of her entire childhood was wiped out because of the crash.

At fourteen years of age, Catherine was made sombre by the knowledge of the fragility of life engendered by the crash. She learnt that life could be taken away very brutally. Having lost her memory temporarily, she began to reflect on 'who she was and what she was'.

Jacqueline, however, felt that the experience of growing up during the war had made them more resilient. They had lived through the war and were acutely conscious of what it took to survive. They were also young so, generally, much more likely to recover quickly.

Physically, the most severely injured took many months to resume their normal lives. Geneviève was on crutches for over six months. Françoise could not tolerate noise, even the sound of her brother bouncing a ball. She was afflicted with headaches for over twelve months and it was several years before she felt restored to good health.

Catherine spent three months on crutches. Micheline was unable to walk unaided for fourteen months. However, as a result of having to change courses at college she met her future husband, so she regarded it as providential.

Except for a few local reports, their return to France was hardly mentioned in the newspapers.

Even so, amongst the girls themselves, there was a sense – and they all felt it – that they had come out of their ordeal incredibly lightly: a feeling that they had survived something immense, by chance or by destiny, and come back to France against the odds.

Whether they would describe it as a miracle depended on the viewpoint of each individual. There were those who felt that God had protected them and this had strengthened their faith and made them more devout. Françoise considered that she had been given extra years by divine intervention. 'It was the road to Damascus,' she said.

Chantal also felt that God was watching over and guiding them during her long walk across the treacherous mountain with Andrée and the pilot. Geneviève spoke of being 'born twice'. A devout Catholic, she still makes regular visits to Lourdes with her mother.

For others, such as Sylvia, it was rather different. No celestial being had interceded on their behalf. Their own obdurate determination to survive had seen them through. They remained unconverted. If anything, they now had a stronger belief in themselves.

Following in the footsteps of her aunts, who were Carmelite nuns, Françoise entered a convent in Valognes three years after the crash. Andrée, Eliane and Odile Lecoquière became teachers. Nicole did not become a dancer, as the doctors predicted, but a teacher of deaf and dumb children. Geneviève took up nursing. Lilette eventually trained to be a doctor. The others devoted themselves to their families.

All of them agreed that their enforced stay in Ireland had been a positive experience, even though none of them, apart from Andrée, had ever returned. They kept wonderful memories of their convalescence and all felt great kindness – the kindness of strangers – in the country.

Lilette, in her own account, wrote:

> For most of us, even the most seriously injured, we did not take away a bad memory of Ireland and that was because, every day for hours on end, we had visitors: VIPs and especially Guides who did ingenious things to please us and make conversation half in English and half in French. We were not likely to forget this indoor 'campfire' given to us by some Irish Guiders.
>
> I sometimes ask myself: should such a similar event occur to Irish Guides visiting France, would the Guides and Eclaireuses have been as nice to them as they were to us?

Following the girls' return to France, there were no attempts to keep in regular contact with each other. Janine remarked:

> Everybody went home and seemed no longer to want to talk about it or to evoke any common memories. In fact I think we were too young to construct a past. The future with its new adventures was more important. It was more important to live rather than relive.

Very soon, the tale of their experience in the 'pelting summer' of 1946 was, as Janine noted, 'tucked away in the drawer of anecdotes'.

The years passed. As time went by, they began to think less and less about their accident – except at odd moments, when the memory surfaced with a strange power in the fragmented way that a dream can sometimes resonate the following day.

Part 3

'A scout saying is "never say die until you are dead." It means a mixture of pluck, patience, and strength.'

Robert Baden-Powell

Forty-one

White Hill is well known to walkers on the Wicklow Way. It's the highest point they have to climb and the path used to be badly maintained. Nowadays a boardwalk, made from railway sleepers, protects the fragile blanket-bog beneath. A saddle joins White Hill to Djouce Mountain and walkers can take a detour to climb up to the cairn at the top of Djouce, from which, on a clear day, the view is one of the finest in County Wicklow.

Known locally as the Barr, the boardwalk then descends via steps into a valley. It passes a stone boulder, a memorial to the founder of the Wicklow Way, J.B. Malone. Near to this point you can look down, past conifers planted by Coillte, onto the dark waters of Lough Tay, where the Luggala estate nestles amongst the trees beside it. On the green carpet of the estate is a decorated ornamental building. It is another stone memorial, to Tara Browne, the youngest son of Oonagh Guinness and Lord Oranmore and Browne. A friend of John Lennon, Tara died in a car accident on the King's Road in Chelsea in 1966 at the age of twenty-one, inspiring the Beatles' song 'A Day in the Life'.

That same year, J.B. Malone published his scheme for a Wicklow Way.

Shortly after the crash, in his 'Irishman's Diary' column in *The Irish Times* on 21 August 1946, Quidnunc had written about the 'pleasure of losing his watch on the shoulder of Djouce'.

> For a moment I thought I might retrace my steps and pry about in the sodden grasses. But there were other people on the mountainside and it would be necessary to explain what had happened. 'Oh, no – but what bad luck. But it must be somewhere. Have you any idea where you lost it?' At the same time their desire would be to get down as quickly as possible from this desolate place, and to leave me, and my watch to the advancing rain. I left it there, with the remnants of an aeroplane.

With time, those remnants gradually disappeared and became part of people's fences and of their memories. Those who had helped to bring down the victims would tell their stories. Pat O'Brien sometimes stopped Garech Browne in Roundwood and talked of how, on the night of the calamity, Garech's father, Lord Oranmore and Browne, had roared into the village from Luggala in his Ford V8 and boomed, 'Are you coming to the rescue?'

The locals told of how they had acted by instinct. It was the same as to sneeze, to blink, to breathe. Locals who had never participated heard the stories so often that they would say, 'Oh yes, I remember.' And in a sense they did, because the stories were so familiar they knew them by heart.

For many years, the site continued to attract locals and the curious. J.B. Malone referred to the incident as 'Wicklow's strangest air crash' and it merited a few lines in guidebooks to the Wicklow Way. In 1993 Michael O'Reilly, an aviation historian, rediscovered a nine-foot section of a wing from the wreckage, which he had originally uncovered in 1981. He subsequently wrote an article for the *North Wicklow Newsround*, recalling the story of the crash.

Bog, heather, water and weathering eventually swallowed up all that the years of souvenir hunting had missed — until nearly fifty years later, when a journalist, Bill Nelson, climbed the now well-trodden path and discovered another stray piece from the plane.

An aviation enthusiast, he set about researching the accident and the history of the Junkers 52.

In a house in Greystones, four women — Eileen Whooley, Muriel Webster, Theresa Moore and Mary Markey — are conversing in French. They meet every week, if possible, in each other's homes to brush up on their French conversational skills. The topics they discuss are wide ranging, from the weather in Ireland to their latest holiday plans. This week, Eileen Whooley has something on her mind.

'*Mais qu'est-ce qu'on fait?*' she asks. She explains that she is trying to find accommodation for at least twelve French women who are planning to visit the country for a few days in May. The women have given her strict instructions to 'be mindful of the fact that they do not wish to spend too much money'.

Elaborating on her story, she tells the others that the French ladies were involved in a plane crash in County Wicklow in 1946 (her friend Gertie found a piece of the plane, by the way) and now they are planning to return to revisit the scene of their ordeal after fifty-two years.

'But I visited those girls in St Bricin's Hospital,' says Muriel Webster (*née* Berry). 'I corresponded with one of them, Jacqueline, for a few years afterwards.' The ladies exclaim what a small world Ireland is. *C'est seulement un village*, they say.

Muriel Webster is still involved in The Irish Girl Guides, a member of the Trefoil Guild ('for 'old' Guides and Guiders'). It isn't long before Eileen Whooley hands over her task to Muriel.

Forty-two

After the events of 1946, Chantal de Vitry returned to Paris and resumed her studies at the Sorbonne. Her parents sold the house in Barbentane, at the confluence of the Rhône and the Durance, after a decision was made to divert the River Durance, thus flooding three-quarters of the de Vitry's land.

Chantal dropped out of her new course in physics because in 1948, at the age of twenty-three, she married Vincent Lacoin.

As the bells had rung out over Paris, dominated by the toll of the great bell of Notre-Dame, after four years of silence, to the refrain of the Marseillaise, her putative husband had marched with de Gaulle in his triumphant parade up the Champs Elysées on 26 August 1944, having successfully liberated one of the last German strongholds in Paris, the Palais du Luxembourg, the day before.

In a country intent on increasing its birth rate after the slaughter of the First World War, Chantal was the eldest of ten children in her family and her husband was the youngest of ten in his.

She moved from her house in the avenue Victor Hugo to her husband's family apartment on the Boulevard Raspail in the seventh *arrondissement*, round the corner from the rue du Bac. The *porte cochère*, the heavy outside door, opened into a beautiful large, covered courtyard and the Lacoin family occupied two floors of the building, high above the noise of traffic on the bustling road.

In this *arrondissement* the first houses of aristocratic Paris had been built during Henry IV's reign. In the sixteenth century, the stones for building the Château des Tuileries had been transported through the rue du Bac. Nowadays the street is most famous for its church, La Chapelle de la Medaille Miraculeuse – home of the Sisters of Saint-Vincent de Paul – and the up-market department store Le Bon Marché.

Time passed. Chantal had nine children and several grandchildren – *une famille nombreuse*.

She had never been back to Ireland but her youngest daughter, Babette, made several trips, staying in Greystones with families that Chantal had befriended in 1946, one of whom was the sister-in-law of Dr Meagher, the young, popular doctor at St Michael's Hospital. During these holidays Babette befriended Seamus, Eileen Whooley's son.

Chance is everything. Many years later, in 1983, when Seamus Whooley, now working for Bord Fáilte, began setting up his stand in Le Bon Marché he little expected to see his old friend Babette walk into the department store. The two friends were delighted to see each other again and Babette invited him back to the family apartment in the Boulevard Raspail.

More than ten years later Babette received a letter from Seamus's mother, Eileen Whooley, enclosing an extract from a Wicklow newspaper. The article, by Bill Nelson, described the events of 12 August 1946 in some detail. It noted the exact location of the crash, the arrival of Chantal at the Mount Maulin Hotel 'drenched through and injured' and the subsequent rescue operation, where the rescuers themselves had got into difficulties, some of them having to 'form human chains, linking each other for support'.

The article pointed out that as a result of many such accidents 'a system called Ground Proximity Warning System was developed. This system, used in conjunction with a radio altimeter, gives aural warnings in the cockpit if an aircraft comes within a preset height of closing terrain.'

The piece ended:

> So that is the story of the Ju-52, AAC I, Toucan. Built and operated by the French. Flown by a French crew, carrying French passengers, coming from France and coincidentally crashing into a mountain with a distinctly French sounding name: Djouce ... This year, 12 August 1996, the fiftieth anniversary, again falls on a Monday.

Chantal read the article over and over. She had held on to the memory of that day of her survival. She had never forgotten the warmth and generosity of the Irish people, from the time she arrived at the Mount Maulin Hotel to the day of the last girls' return to France. It had not, however, occurred to her that the anniversary of the accident would be acknowledged in Ireland after half a century. She was so excited anyone in Ireland had remembered the incident that she did not want to keep the news simply to herself.

It took nearly two years to track down the other survivors, *les rescapées*.

The job was made harder because not only had most of 'the girls' married and changed their names but also many of the addresses from 1946 had been temporary summer residences of which there was no record.

Lilette was still living in the family apartment in the rue Raffet and had realised her dream of becoming a doctor.

Thanks to the encouragement of her husband, she had completed the years of study after she married. She was pregnant with her fourth child when she eventually qualified.

One of the most difficult to track down was Eliane Lemonnier, one of *les trois valides*. Antoinette Grandguillot (*née* Emo) and her husband started looking in Equeurdreville, the village near Cherbourg where Eliane came from. They asked every person in the village and, eventually, their perseverence paid off. They discovered that she had married a garage owner and moved to Paris. Chantal and Anne began to search every garage in Paris on foot. After many false leads, they were told that there was an old, established family-owned garage called Royer at the Filles du Calvaire métro station near the Bastille.

Disturbing a man working under a car, they enquired after Eliane Lemonnier. The man shot out. Lying on the ground, half on his side, he said: 'That's my mother! She's working upstairs.' Eliane Royer looked after the books for the family business.

Micheline was the last to be found. She had moved from Vincennes, was married with children and grandchildren and was living in La Trinité sur Mer in Brittany.

Their search had finally come to an end.

Of the original twenty-one Guides de France and Eclaireuses, twenty were still alive. Odile Stahlberger had died from cancer in 1995, leaving two children.

Only one of the crew was still living, the wireless operator Daniel Duran, now confined to a wheelchair and living in Gontaud de Nogaret in the Lot et Garonne *département*.

Apart from Françoise Béchet, the others were married with children and grandchildren and scattered all over France. They found Andrée in Issoire, Ginette in Nantes and three of the Le Havre girls – Jacqueline, Antoinette (Emo) and Odile (Lecoquière) – still in Le Havre. The town had been completely reconstructed since the war, with blocks of flats built to a common height on a uniform structural grid, which Anne (Lemmonier) thought was '*horrible*'.

Living in Paris were Agnès, Catherine, Anne, Eliane and Sylvia. Close by, in Saint Germaine en Laye, was Janine. Magali had moved to Versailles.

Antoinette (Nattier) had settled in the rebuilt town of Saint Lô, Geneviève in Rouen. Nicole had moved to Lille and Monique, originally from Sainte Mère Eglise, was living in Perpignan in the South of France.

It soon transpired that not only Chantal had felt the event had been a defining moment in their lives. What also became evident was that they had kept alive the good memories of their stay in Ireland and some, like Antoinette (Nattier), were astonished at how vividly they remembered certain details. After five decades, they were anxious to share their anecdotes and get together again. The idea of going back to Ireland on what they would call 'a pilgrimage' soon took root.

Janine had some reservations. To her it was strange. Having kept their silence for fifty years with no contact whatsoever, why bother to meet again now? Many years after the accident she had recounted the story to 'astonished friends and grandchildren', but there had been no attempt to share this with the other survivors during all this time.

Andrée, Eliane and Catherine retained a fear of flying but, for family or work reasons, they had been obliged to use this form of transport. Nicole's initial fears, when she would grip her husband's wrist on take off, were overcome when she started to bring her grandchildren on holidays. Now she quite enjoyed flying and felt she was 'vaccinated' against having another crash. Antoinette (Emo) also felt she was protected by the laws of statistics and her lucky stars. The others, including Ginette, were totally at ease with flying now.

As far as shaping their futures, Janine was sceptical. She

was not sure that the event had had any determining effect on her life.

On the contrary, Odile (Lecoquière) felt strongly that it had helped to forge her character: having already had to cope with living through the war years, this next tribulation, she felt, helped to prepare her for future trials. As somebody had said to her recently: '*Vous vous en êtes plutôt bien tirée*' — You really came out of it well, considering.

Françoise Béchet regarded it as an enriching experience but added a caveat: 'When there are serious accidents, I say — above all understand that you will not find your husband or your children as before. It changes you completely.'

Forty-three

In September 1997 Chantal wrote to Muriel Webster telling her that she had tracked down seventeen of the Guides and there were now only 'four missing'. Their plan was to make a pilgrimage to the scene of the crash, to visit St Michael's and St Bricin's hospitals and to meet up, if possible, with some of the Girl Guides and 'Captains' who had been 'so nice to the injured girls' in 1946.

Through her contacts with The Irish Girl Guides, Muriel managed to book the Bunk Room of the Guide cottage in Enniskerry for their stay, which was arranged for May of the following year. She then contacted five of the 'old girls' who had either been at the camp in Rathfarnham in 1946 or visited the girls in hospital. Together, they formed an organising committee for the visit, composed of Anne Bowen, Dorothy Mills, Anne Turbett, Vera Pepper, Gladys James, Muriel Webster and Margaret Hamilton-Reid, then eighty-five years old.

The organisers set about contacting as many people as possible who might have memories of the event. They also put together a press release for the media.

It had been Whitsun in 1946 when Margaret Hamilton-Reid had first travelled to France, by boat and train with Mrs

Lillis, the Area Commissioner for Dublin, and Ethel Moore, the International Commissioner, and the initial plans for the French visit had been formalised. It would be Whitsun fifty-two years later when some of the French 'girls' would return to Ireland for what was hoped would be a happier occasion.

With over half a century of living etched on their figures and faces, in October 1997 thirteen of the French survivors got together in Paris for the first time in fifty-one years.

On 2 June 1998, Dermot James wrote in 'An Irishman's Diary' in *The Irish Times*:

> It does not often happen that when a plane crashes into a mountain, everybody in the aircraft survives the ordeal. It happens even less often that more than half the survivors of such an accident would want, fifty-two years later, to revisit the site of the crash and to say thank you to those who rescued them and cared for them in hospital. Yet this is exactly what has been happening this weekend and the story is worth telling in some detail.

Waiting at Dublin Airport for the Aer Lingus flight to touch down on 30 May 1998 were Eileen Whooley, Anne Bowen, Muriel Webster and a researcher for RTÉ radio with bright red hair.

The ladies had chatted ebulliently on the plane. They talked about their families, their children and their many grandchildren. They discussed why they had been chosen for the holiday in Ireland in the first place. Of all the thousands of Guides and Girl Scouts in France, and from the *villes martyres*, they wondered why they in particular had been singled out for the ill-fated trip.

'Perhaps I was chosen because of my dynamism,' Catherine laughed.

'I think I was just free at the time,' said Lilette, shrugging.

Whatever the reasons, it seemed chance had thrown them together – chance and its agents: time and place.

They joked about the first time the Guides de France had met in Madame de Beaulieu's sitting-room in the avenue Victor Hugo on the eve of the flight, when the air was filled with such excitement and expectation.

Adjusting the scarf round her neck, seventy-three-year-old Chantal Lacoin led the pilgrims through the parting doors of the arrivals hall of Dublin Airport. Behind her followed Lilette Lemoine, Andrée Brocard, Catherine Bertier, Geneviève Carrière, Monique Divetain, Antoinette Grandguillot, Odile Longour, Nicole Lucquin, Anne Parez, Jacqueline Plottin and Agnès Vallin.

There in spirit were Eliane Royer, Sylvia Ostrowetsky, Ginette Rogier, Janine Fistel, Antoinette Roudot, Françoise Béchet, Magali Petitmengin and Micheline Huré.

Before the French party walked into the foyer, the parting words of Madame de Beaulieu that balmy Sunday evening in August 1946 echoed down the years: 'Above all do not forget that you are representing France.'

'They all came out wearing neckerchiefs,' said Eileen Whooley. 'They were laughing, radiant. I've never seen a group of people so animated in my life.'

During their three days in Dublin, they slept in sleeping-bags in the Bunk Room of the Guide cottage in Enniskerry and had bread and instant coffee for breakfast. They were Girl Guides again for the weekend.

Margaret Hamilton-Reid hosted a dinner for them. Moira Cooke presented them each with a drawing as a memento of their trip. One of the Irish Girl Guides produced a cake with the Irish and French flags iced on the top.

They visited St Michael's Hospital and St Bricin's. At St Bricin's, they received a warm welcome from the commanding officer, Lieutenant Colonel Browne. The French flag was flying. He said:

> It is very pleasant to welcome you to St Bricin's Hospital, particularly the five of you who were patients here between 13 August and 10 September 1946. It is wonderful that you have come back after fifty-two years. Most of the doctors and nurses who were here in 1946 are very old or dead but two doctors who remember you have come here this morning to see you again.

They were Lieutenant Colonel McGoldrick and Colonel Joseph Laffan who, on 13 August 1946, had recorded in his diary the commotion their admission had caused.

Colonel Browne showed the women Ward One – completely unchanged since 1946. The military authorities had a habit of holding on to all of their records and Colonel Browne finally presented Catherine, Nicole, Antoinette, Jacqueline and Lilette with a copy of their medical notes, 'as a souvenir of your stay here'.

On Sunday morning, under grey skies, the Guides de France attended a mass in Enniskerry, where another French tricolour had been hoisted in the church. The flowers were red, white and blue. The priest included 'a special thought' in his prayers for all the survivors. They were reunited with more Irish Girl Guides who had visited them in hospital, including Sea Rangers Betty Halpin, Myra Healey, Betty O'Connor and Mona Heary.

As the clouds began to break up and patches of blue sky appeared, they travelled by coach along the old Long Hill Road towards Roundwood through the townland of Ballinastoe. Fifty-two years earlier Billy Deely, Conor Hogan and Norman Keegan from Enniskerry had set out from here in the driving rain and had arguably been the first to locate the plane.

The driver parked the coach on the Sally Gap Road overlooking Lough Tay. Djouce Mountain was behind them.

As well as the RTÉ cameramen, the *Nationwide* reporters and the researcher, Dr Meagher and his wife had come out to meet 'Dr Meagher's Girls' again. There was an emotional reunion with Anne Lemonnier, Geneviève and Antoinette Emo, whom he had looked after with unstinting care for six long weeks, from 12 August to 21 October.

The ladies looked across to the Fancy Rock above Lough Tay and could discern the gothic pile of Luggala nestling in the trees, now restored by Lord Oranmore and Browne's son Garech Browne. Fifty-two years earlier, the wireless operator Daniel Duran and the navigator Michel Tourret from the stricken Junkers 52 had stumbled into the garden as darkness fell, astonishing members of the family after dinner.

Lord Oranmore and Browne sent a telegram and telephoned from London. He regretted that he could not be there to meet the ladies once again. A bouquet of flowers from his son Garech arrived at the Guide cottage.

MESSAGE FROM LORD ORANMORE AND BROWNE, London

Lord and Lady Oranmore and Browne were in residence in Luggala at the time of the crash and rendered assistance.

His Lordship is very sorry that he cannot meet with the French Party and sends them all good wishes.

He is now 97 years of age.

Members of the Roundwood Historical Society extended a '*Céad Míle Fáilte*' to the French Girl Guides on 'this unique and historic occasion' and recounted some local anecdotes about the crash, which had become part of the local folklore. The survivors were escorted to the ruin of the Sheepbank House near the Boleyhorrigan Bridge, evoking memories of hot milky tea, whiskey from the bottle and the smell of fragrant burning peat.

The distinguished names associated with the Guide movement from its beginning were long dead, including Lady Powerscourt, the first Chief Commissioner of The Irish Girl Guides, and Ethel Moore, the International Commissioner. The Guide cottage in Enniskerry, conceived after the death of B.P., had opened in 1950. The Chief Guide, Lady B.P., died in 1977. Eileen Beatty was the Chief Commissioner of The Irish Girl Guides from 1957 until 1970. Thereafter she was President until her death in 1980. In 1994, Madame de Beaulieu died, donating her body to science.

The journalist Patrick Campbell, who as Quidnunc had written the 'Irishman's Diary' pieces for *The Irish Times*, left Ireland to work in London in 1947. 'From my earliest days,' he said, 'I have enjoyed an attractive impediment in my speech.' He later turned this to his advantage on the BBC programme *Call My Bluff*, seen by millions. Later he moved to the South of France, where he died in 1980.

Brothers Conor and Brian Hogan were both dead. Brian's son Mark later said that his father, who passed away in 1997, would have loved to have been at the reunion. He had never forgotten the girl who had arrived at the Mount Maulin Hotel in a 'pitiable condition' and often talked about 'Chantal de Vitry' and the year of the 'bad harvest'. The house, no longer a hotel, had changed little from those days when Mr and Mrs Hogan welcomed guests into their lounge and the conversation flowed.

Oonagh Guinness divorced Lord Oranmore and Browne in 1950 and went on to marry the Spanish fashion designer Miquel Ferraras, while Lord Oranmore married the actress Sally Gray. On 2 August 1995 – the same day as her daughter Tessa Kindersley's tragic death in 1946 at the age of fourteen – Oonagh died.

Sergeant McNally was also dead, as was Sergeant Wickham after serving thirty-two years and eleven days in An Garda Síochána.

The elderly artist couple, Mr and Mrs Davis, died in the fifties and their cottage in the Deerpark was demolished soon after to make way for the visitors' centre that now stands at the foot of the Powerscourt Waterfall.

At the time of the reunion, Bill Deely, Charlie Keegan and Paul Rowan were still alive, as was Arthur Tomkins, who had heard the plane flying low over his beach hut near Jack's Hole. He could recall the day clearly and was prompted to write to Dermot James after he read his 'Irishman's Diary' piece.

'I have had to turn my hand to typing because in my old age — ninety-eight this month — my handwriting has so deteriorated that I can hardly decipher it myself.'

As the Eclaireuses climbed down from the coach on the Sally Gap Road — Cheftaine Lilette Levy-Bruhl and Eclaireuse Nicole Jacques-Léon — followed by the Guides de France — Cheftaines Chantal de Vitry and Andrée Bonnet, and Guides Geneviève Bétrancourt, Anne Lemonnier, Antoinette Emo, Catherine de Geuser, Agnès Laporte, Odile Lecoquière, Monique Ygouf and Jacqueline Conort — two older men with grey, thinning hair stepped out of the crowd.

In 1946, amidst much newspaper coverage, the *Irish Independent* had run the story in its editorial:

> Mention should be made of the energy with which the rescue parties discharged their work. Those who know how difficult it is to find their way across the Wicklow Hills, no easy task even in daylight, will appreciate the achievement of finding the wrecked plane, and the dangers that the rescuers faced in mist and heavy rain. We may be proud of those who brought aid so quickly when it was sorely needed.

One of those rescuers, Pa Brennan, his once broad shoulders slightly shrunk, had come back to shake the hands of the girls he had helped to carry down the mountain fifty-two years before. In his other hand he held a Players untipped cigarette.

'Where's Jacqueline?' said the other, more slightly built figure, looking from face to face.

Pat O'Brien, the turf cutter from Roundwood, was reunited with Jacqueline Conort from Le Havre. 'You had a little medallion round your neck with "Jacqueline" engraved on it,' he said, his eyes welling.

In St Bricin's Hospital in 1946, Jacqueline, who had hardly ever cried before, wept when she heard the sound of Chopin's 'Funeral March' playing in Ward One. Now in the arms of Pat O'Brien, fifty-two years later, once again Jacqueline's face was streaked with tears.

The French Guides then followed the boardwalk along the Barr past J.B. Malone's memorial stone to see for themselves where their ordeal had started on the soft, boggy ground all those years ago.

For the first time, they were able to realise what an extraordinary set of circumstances had combined to help avert a tragedy: the weather, which had been their undoing but which had also proved to be their salvation, softening the ground even more than usual; the mountain, with its liberal supply of moss and heather, which had acted as a cushion and enabled the pilot to make a belly landing on a gradual slope; the sturdy aircraft, whose three engines had been shorn off, thus preventing a fire, and which had not disintegrated on impact, providing a refuge for the survivors during their long wait through the night – the night when the last of the survivors to come down the mountain had seen the mysterious, elusive flickering lights on the ground, the *feux follets*, and the misty constellations in the sky.

It's a tough walk from Luggala to Djouce Mountain and Dorothy Mills (*née* Jolley), a Guide at the Rathfarnham camp in 1946, escorted them part of the way.

> We did not get the whole way as most of the French ladies were not experienced hill walkers and did not really have suitable footwear, but we were very close and they were able to see the rest of the way up.

Against a backdrop of Djouce Mountain, with the blue-brown domes of Wicklow stretching into the distance, the ladies turned as a group southward towards the dark waters of Lough Tay, which mirrored the Fancy Rock and the high drifting clouds. Towards the east they could see the Great Sugarloaf or Slieve Cualainn beyond the sheet of water of the Vartry Reservoir. For a moment they stood in silence and remembered. For a moment they let their spirits mingle with the spirits of the mountain. Then Nicole started to sing – quietly at first, the others taking up the theme:

> *Quoi qu'il m'arrive*
> *J'ai toujours le sourire*

And then, linking arms, they sang with more energy and passion:

> *Je prends la vie, les choses du bon coté*
> *En me disant qu'il peut arriver pire*
> *Et ça suffit pour me mettre en gaité.*

Forty-four

5 June 1998, County Clare

Cher Committee,

We have been enthralled with the Burren and Connemara
and we'll take back wonderful memories of your beautiful
island. We realise we have been lucky to crash on Mount
Djouce and not in the Burren. We have felt as young as
fifty-two years ago thanks to your warm welcome.

Love from,

Chantal, Geneviève, Antoinette, Jacqueline, Nicole,
Catherine, Andrée, Monique, Lilette, Odile, Agnès, Anne

Nicole recalled that Chantal wore her Guide scarf for the
entire trip. Afterwards, in a letter to Muriel Webster, Chantal
expressed all their feelings:

> We will never forget our weekend with you ... We will never
> know how to thank you and the committee for allowing us
> to be all together in the marvellous Irish Girl Guide cottage
> and so to know each other; to discover Djouce Mountain
> and to realise how lucky we are to be here.

Since their reunion they all talk about their accident much
more often. It has brought them together. After all the years

of separation, 'we became friends', Lilette says. 'Even though we hadn't seen each other for so many intervening years, we had survived something together; we had shared the same adventure.' They were entrusted to one another when they were young, in the days that mattered. The friends of our youth are perhaps the only people who know us properly.

Anne loves to meet up with the other 'girls' from Le Havre and listen to their stories. 'They are my memory now,' she says.

Most of the women have held on to photographs and press cuttings from 1946 and turned them into scrapbooks and albums, '*nos souvenirs*'. They make an impressive record as those of Geneviève and Agnès attest. Nicole has a huge dossier: '*C'est mon trésor*,' she says, clutching it to her chest.

Les rescapées meet as often as they can, sometimes at Lilette's apartment in the rue Raffet, other times, when they feel like getting out of Paris, at Micheline's house on the Brittany coast or Monique's in Perpignan. Their passion for life remains undiminished, perhaps because they came so perilously close to losing it.

'When we meet, we are like old war veterans,' says Lilette. 'We drink, we eat, we laugh about old times.'

Les anciennes combattantes show off their war wounds. Nicole pulls up her trouser leg to reveal a tremendous scar on her right knee. When a nurse suggested recently that she have some cosmetic surgery, she said, pulling away her leg in outrage, 'Nobody is touching that. It's an historic monument.'

'So you see, life continued,' says Geneviève blithely, 'because I'm still here – *puisque je suis toujours là*.'

And Janine's grandchildren tell all their astonished friends, as their eyes widen into circles: '*Vous vous rendez compte: une mamie qui a eu un accident d'avion, ça c'est quelque chose!*' – Do you realise we have a grandmother who was in a plane crash? Now that really *is* something!

❧

Far away, across the Irish Sea, where the mountains make their own weather, the sky suddenly darkens. The rain comes down in sheets. It falls on Djouce, Lough Tay and over the Glensoulan Valley; and it rattles like a shower of pebbles on the roof of a hen house in Ballinastoe.

Postscript

During the writing of this book, the deaths unfortunately occurred of Charlie Keegan, Sylvia Ostrowetsky, Moira Cooke, Dan Nolan and Arthur Tomkins.

Sylvia, *la Benjamine*, passed away in April 2004 after a long struggle with cancer. She was seventy-one years old. Catherine Bertier (de Geuser) represented *les réscapées* at her funeral amidst many tributes. Her interment took place in Père Lachaise cemetery in Paris.

France under the Occupation

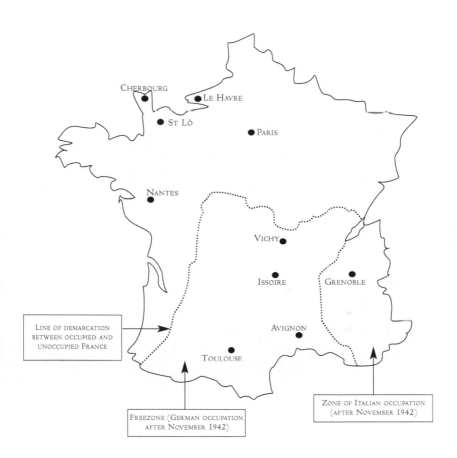

CHERBOURG

LE HAVRE

ST LÔ

PARIS

NANTES

VICHY

ISSOIRE

GRENOBLE

AVIGNON

Line of demarcation
between occupied and
unoccupied France

TOULOUSE

Zone of Italian occupation
(after November 1942)

Freezone (German occupation
after November 1942)

PROBABLE COURSE OF THE JUNKERS 52

Maps

Area surrounding the crasii site

In August 1946 magnetic declination in the Dublin area was approximately 13.5° West of North

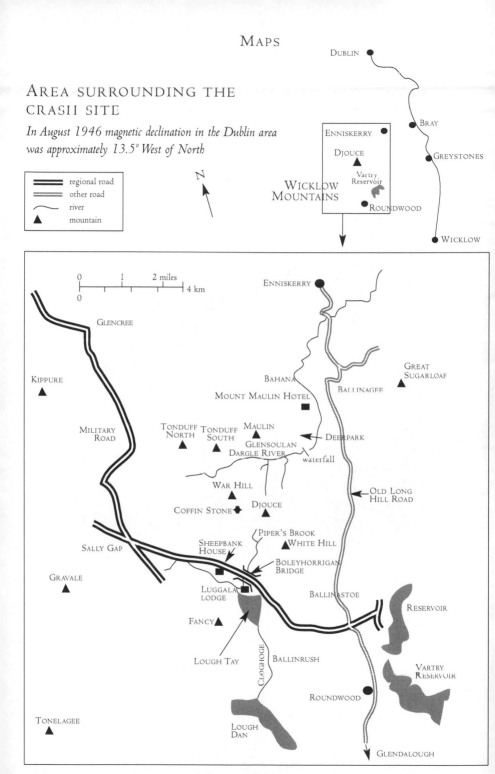

TECHNICAL DETAILS OF JU-52/3M, *TANTE JU*

Wingspan	29.25 m
Length	18.90 m
Height	4.50 m
Wings surface	110.5 sq m
Weight empty	5,900 kg
MTOW	10,500 kg
Freight	4,100 kg
Maximum speed	270 km/h
Cruise speed	200 km/h
Landing speed	100 km/h
Ceiling	5,500 m
Service range	915 km
Maximum range	1,280 km
Passengers	16
Engines	3 x BMW 132A
Number of cylinders	9 radial
Weight	530 kg
Power	660 hp
Engine capacity	27.7 l
Compression ratio	6.93:1
Fuel consumption	220g/hp/h
Propeller	2 blades, with variable angle
Year of construction	1939

Extract from Wireless Operator's Log

PROCÈS-VERBAL D'EXPLOITATION RADIOTÉLÉGRAPHIQUE

177B   Opérateur: Adjt. Duran   Date: 12/8/'46.

Heure (TMG)	Appel		Radiotelegramme et Indication de fin D'Emission
	R	de	E.
0808	FNB	7B	QAD FNB 0802z QAB Dublin
	7B	B	R K
30	FDT3	7B	TR K
			R K
38	FNB	7B	NW QBG 1500 QTI 300 K
	7B	B	R 1500 Metres ou feet? K
			MTR K
43	FNF	7B	TR - a 0835 QTH 4928N 0136E QTJ 250
			QTI 309 QAH 1800 MTR ASC 2200 K
	7B	FMF	R K
0905	FNB	7B	QDR?
		NB	319 K
10	MVU	7B	TR NW QTH St. Valery QTI 309 QBF 2200 K
	7B	MVU	R K
15	FNB	7B	NW QSO MVU K VA
22	FDT	7B	QTO NR1 a 0920z - JU 52 NR 46 a Rabelais
			Vigoureux Bernadotte - a 0910 QTH
			St. Valery

Transcript of Wireless Operator's Log

0808: <u>from 7B to Le Bourget</u> (335 kHz channel)
Left Le Bourget at 0802. May I have clearance for Dublin?
<u>Le Bourget to 7B</u>
Affirmation.

0830: <u>from 7B to Le B</u> (6015 kHz channel)
TR & R [seems to be just a check of the channel].

0838: <u>from 7B to Le B</u> (335 kHz channel)
I am flying above cloud at 1500. My true track [i.e. with respect to true north] is 300°.
<u>Le B to 7B</u>
1500 metres or feet?
<u>Reply</u>
Metres.

0843: <u>from 7B to Beauvais</u>
At 0835, position was 49° 28 N, 01° 36 E.
My speed is 250 km/hr. True course 309°.
Altitude 1800 metres, ascending to 2200.

0905: <u>from 7B to Beauvais</u>
Request QDR [i.e. magnetic bearing from you] from Beauvais.
<u>Reply</u>
QDR is 319°.

0910: <u>from 7B to Uxbridge</u>
Position Saint Valery. My true track is 302°. Flying in cloud at 2200 metres. [Acknowledged by Uxbridge.]

0915: <u>from 7B to Le B</u> (335 kHz channel)
Flying north-west. Can you communicate directly with Uxbridge?

0922: <u>from 7B to Chartres</u>
I have messages for you.
At 0920 GMT, Ju52, number 046 going to Rabelais, Vigaureux, Bernadotte – at 0910 was over Saint Valery. Speed 150 km/h. True

track 309°. Flying over cloud at 2200 metres. Will you relay [free of charge to Le B 6015 kHz channel]?

From Chartres to 7B

Yes, I will relay to Le B (6015 kHz channel).

09??: from 7B to Le B (4195 kHz channel).

I have the following message to send: Since the meteorological report from Le B, the meteorological conditions as observed from aircraft over the Channel at 0940 GMT. Clouded, the amount, type and height of the base of the cloud is 4 to 5/10. Stratocumulus base 1000 twice as much 3/10. Altocumulus and altostratus base 3500/4000. Horizontal visibility 20 km. Wind direction and speed between 2000 and 2500. West 60 to 80 km/h

From Le B (4195 kHz channel) to 7B

Roger. I acknowledge receipt of message.

1000: Uxbridge (33kHz) from 7B

What is the name of the Gonio (direction finder) at Dublin?

7B from Uxbridge

What is your position [in latitude and longitude]? What is your height?

Uxbridge from 7B

NW. Overhead Isle of Wight. Flying in visual met. Conditions at 2200 metres.

Uxbridge to 7B

Roger.

1003: Uxbridge to 7B

Gonio Dublin EIJ 405 kHz.

7B to Uxbridge

Roger.

1008: Uxbridge to 7B

Change your transmission frequency to the frequency of GJB.

7B to Uxbridge

Roger. What is the name of the station?

Uxbridge to 7B

Bristol.

1045: 7B to Manchester

TR.

<u>Manchester to 7B</u>
Roger. Can you transmit directly to EIJ?
<u>7B to Manchester</u>
Roger.

1115: <u>Manchester from 7B</u>
QTE? [My true bearing from you.]
<u>7B from Manchester</u>
200.

1135: <u>Dublin/EIJ from 7B</u>
TR- QAA ABF 1315 GMT QDM?
<u>7B from Dublin</u>
QDM 325°.
<u>Dublin from 7B</u>
Roger. What is the surface wind direction and speed?
<u>7B from Dublin</u>
Asc.

1145: <u>Dublin from 7B</u>
I am flying in cloud. DESC.
My radio is suffering interference 5/5.

1200: <u>7B from Dublin</u>
Surface wind direction and speed 28 m.p.h. gusting to 40 m.p.h..
Altimetre setting 990.7 millibars.
Horizontal visibility at 1200 GMT: 3 miles. Cloud base height
300 feet 7/10.
The magnetic direction of the runway to be used is 006.
<u>Dublin from 7B</u>
Will you indicate the magnetic heading for me to steer towards
you?
<u>7B from Dublin</u>
334°.

1218: <u>7B from Dublin</u>
What is your height?
<u>Dublin from 7B</u>
680 metres.

SOME IMPORTANT DATES IN THE HISTORY OF GUIDING IN IRELAND AND FRANCE

1857   Robert Baden-Powell (B.P.) is born on 22 February

1889   Olave St Clair Soames is born on 22 February

1907   B.P. organises an experimental camp on Brownsea Island, Dorset, for twenty-one boys

1908   *Scouting for Boys* is published

1910   The Girl Guides Association is formed. Agnes Baden-Powell is President

1911   The first Irish Girl Guide company is started in Harold's Cross, Dublin. The Association of Eclaireurs of France (EDF) – a Boy Scout movement – is founded

1912   Robert Baden-Powell marries Olave Soames

1914   The first sections of the Eclaireuses – Girl Scouts – are created

1918   Lady Baden-Powell is appointed Chief Guide

1920   The first World Conference is held in England

1923   The Guides de France is founded. The first Guide is Odette Lenain

1928   Lord and Lady B.P. visit Dublin and the first swimming gala is held at Iveagh Baths, Dublin. The World Association of Girl Guides and Girl Scouts (WAGGGS) is set up and the World Bureau opens in London. A Catholic Girl Guide Association called Clanna Bríde is established in Ireland

1929   Lady Powerscourt is appointed Chief Commissioner of The Irish Girl Guides. The organisation is now called The Irish Free State Girl Guides

1930   The World Flag is adopted. Lady Baden-Powell is appointed World Chief Guide

1932   The Irish Free State Girl Guides become members of the WAGGGS for Ireland

1933   The Clanna Bríde title is changed to Bantreoraithe Catoilicí na hÉireann – Catholic Girl Guides of Ireland

1937   Queen Elizabeth is enrolled as a Guide and Princess Margaret is enrolled as a Brownie

1938   The Irish Free State becomes known as Éire and the IFSGG is changed to The Irish Girl Guides. The Irish Tenderfoot Badge – the Celtic knot and the initials IGG – is chosen. Mrs Leigh White from Cork is appointed Director of the World Bureau

1939   The War. Many Guides de France and Eclaireuses are evacuated.

Many continue to meet clandestinely or are involved in the Resistance

1940 All the French Guide and Scout movements are regrouped under the name Scoutisme Français

1941 B.P. dies at Nyeri, Kenya

1943 Trefoil Guild starts for those members of the movement aged over twenty-one. It is decided to build a memorial cottage for B.P. at Enniskerry, Co. Wicklow

1946 The World Badge is adopted at the eleventh World Conference in France. Lady B.P. visits Dublin. Death of Irish Chief Commissioner Lady Powerscourt

1977 Death of the Chief Guide, Lady B.P.

USEFUL ADDRESSES

LES GUIDES DE FRANCE
65, rue de la Glacière - 75013 Paris
Phone: +33 1 47078559
E-mail: acc@guidesdefrance.asso.fr
Web site: www.guidesdefrance.org

ECLAIREUSES ECLAIREURS DE FRANCE
12, place Georges Pompidou
93167 Noisy-le-Grand Cedex
Phone: +33 1 48151766
Fax: +33 1 48151760
E-mail: national@eedf.asso.fr
Web site: www.eedf.asso.fr

THE IRISH GIRL GUIDES
27 Pembroke Park, Dublin 4
Phone: +353 1 6683898
Fax: +353 1 6602779
E-mail: info@irishgirlguides.ie
Web site: www.irishgirlguides.ie

COUNCIL OF IRISH GUIDING ASSOCIATIONS (CIGA)
c/o 27 Pembroke Park
Dublin 4

CATHOLIC GUIDES OF IRELAND
12 Clanwilliam Terrace
Grand Canal Quay
Dublin 2
Phone: +353 1 6619566
Fax: +353 1 6765691
E-mail: nat.office@girlguidesireland.ie
Web site: www.girlguidesireland.ie

SCOUTING NEDERLAND
Postbus 210
3830 AE Leusden
Netherlands

Phone: +31 33 4960911
Fax: +31 33 4960222
E-mail: info@scouting.nl
Web site: www.scouting.nl

WORLD ASSOCIATION OF GIRL GUIDES AND GIRL SCOUTS WORLD BUREAU
Olave Centre
12c Lyndhurst Road
London
NW3 5PQ
England
Phone: +44 20 7794 1181
Fax: +44 20 7431 3764
E-mail: wagggs@wagggsworld.org
Web site: www.wagggsworld.org

GIRLGUIDING UK
17–19 Buckingham Palace Road
London
SW1W 0PT
Phone: +44 207 8346242
Fax: +44 207 828 8317
E-mail: website@girlguiding.org.uk
Web site: www.girlguiding.org.uk

DUBLIN TOURISM
Phone: +353 1 6057700
Web site: www.visitdublin.com

WICKLOW TOURIST OFFICE
Phone: +353 404 20100
Fax: +353 404 67792
E-mail: cosec@wicklowcoco.ie
Web site: www.wicklow.ie

WICKLOW MOUNTAINS NATIONAL PARK INFORMATION OFFICE
Phone: +353 404 45425
Fax: +353 404 45710
Web site: www.heritageireland.ie

Appendix 4

Wicklow Mountains National Park HQ
Phone: +353 404 45800
E-mail: wmnp@duchas.ie
Web site: www.wicklowtourist.com

Mountain Rescue
Phone: 999 or 112

Powerscourt Estate
Web site: www.powerscourt.ie

Heritage Ireland Information
Web site: www.heritageireland.info/djoucemountain/
E-mail: ancient@heritageireland.info

Bibliography

Allen, G., *The Garda Síochána*, Gill & Macmillan, 1999

Beckett, S., *Collected Poems in English and French*, John Calder, 1961

Bellamy, D., *Bellamy's Ireland – Wild Boglands*, Country House, 1987

Bence-Jones, M., *Burke's Guide to Country Houses, Vol. 1 Ireland*, Burke's Peerage, 1978

Bentley, J., *Normandy*, Aurum Press Ltd., 1989

Boylan, H., *Dictionary of Irish Biography*, Gill & Macmillan, 1998

Brophy, J. and A. Flynn, *Book of Wicklow*, Kestrel Books, 1991

Brown, H., *Hamish's Groats End Walk*, Victor Gollancz, 1981

Brown, H. (ed.), *Speak to the Hills*, Aberdeen University Press, 1985

Bulfin, W., *Rambles in Éirinn*, M.H. Gill & Son, 1907

Burke, B., *Burke's Landed Gentry of Ireland*, Burke's Peerage, 1958

Burke, B., *Burke's Peerage and Baronetage*, Burke's Peerage, 1999

Campbell, P., *An Irishman's Diary*, Cassell, 1950

Campbell, P., *My Life and Easy Times*, Anthony Blond, 1967

Davies, P.J., *France and the Second World War*, Routledge, 2000

Donnelly, B., *For the Betterment of the People: A History of Wicklow County Council, 1898–1999*, Wicklow County Council, 1999

Doran, A.L., *Bray and Environs*, Kestrel Books, 1985

Dwyer, T.R., *Guests of the State*, Brandon, 1994

Fewer, M., *A Walk in Ireland*, Atrium, 2000

Fewer, M., *The Wicklow Way*, Gill & Macmillan, 1996

Fisk, R., *In Time of War*, Paladin, 1985

Furedi, F., *Therapy Culture*, Routledge, 2004

Bibliography

Gaffney, P., *Healing Amid the Ruins – The Irish Hospital at Saint-Lô*, A & A Farmar, 1999

Gwynn, E. (ed.), *Metrical Dindsenchas: Royal Irish Academy Todd Lecture Series, Vol. X*, Hodges Figgis & Co., 1913

Grob-Fitzgibbon, B., *The Irish Experience During the Second World War*, Irish Academic Press, 2004

Grogan, E. and T. Hillery, *Guide to the Archaeology of County Wicklow*, Wicklow County Tourism, 1993

Hall, J.S. (ed.), *Radar Aids to Navigation*, McGraw-Hill, 1947

Hannigan, K., and W. Nolan (eds), *Wicklow – History and Society*, Geography Publications, 1994

Herman, D., *Hill Strolls around Dublin*, Reprint Ltd, 1984

Herman, D., *Hill Walker's Wicklow*, Shanksmare Publications, 1989

Heverin, A., *Irish Countrywomen's Association: A History*, Wolfhound Press, 2000

Holland, C.H., *Geology of Ireland*, Dunedin Academic Press, 2001

Joyce, P.W., *Irish Names of Places*, Phoenix Publications, 1913

Kladstrup, D. and P., *Wine and War*, Hodder and Stoughton, 2001

Lewis, S., *Topographical Dictionary of Ireland*, S. Lewis, 1839

Lloyd Praeger, R., *The Way That I Went*, Hodges Figgis, 1937

MacCarron, D., *Landfall Ireland*, Colourpoint Books, 2003

Malone, J.B., *The Complete Wicklow Way*, O'Brien Press, 1990

Malone, J.B., *Walking in Wicklow*, Helicon Ltd, 1964

McCormick, P.J., *The Higher Lakes of Wicklow*, Phylax Press, 1994

Mitchell, F., *Shell Guide to Reading the Irish Landscape*, Country House, 1986

Mitton, J., *Cambridge Dictionary of Astronomy*, Cambridge University Press, 2001

Montague (ed.), *Annual Register for the Year 1946*, Longman's, Green & Co., 1947

Nairne, R., *Discovering Wild Wicklow*, Country House, 2001

Nossiter, A., *France and the Nazis*, Methuen, 2001

Oram, H., *Dublin Airport – The History*, Aer Rianta, 1990

Ostrowetsky, S., *Quelqu'un ou le Livre de Moishe*, Editions Kimé, 1995

O'Sullivan, R.W., *An Irishman's Aviation Sketchbook*, Irish Aviator, 1988

Ousby, I., *Occupation*, John Murray, 1997

Pilcher, J. and V. Hall, *Flora Hibernica*, Collins Press, 2001

Price, L., *Place Names of County Wicklow*, Dublin Institute for Advanced Studies, 1946

Quinn, J., *Down in a Free State: WWII (I)*, WG, 1998

Rayner, J., *Stardust Falling*, Doubleday, 2002

Smith, R.A., *Radio Aids to Navigation*, Cambridge University Press, 1947

Bibliography

Snell, G., *Amy Johnson*, Hodder and Stoughton, 1980

Thoms Directory: 1946, Alex Thom and Co. Ltd, 1947

Tocnaye, Le Chevalier de la, *A Frenchman's Walk through Ireland 1796–7*, Blackstaff Press, 1984

Wall, Claude, *Diaries*, National Library of Ireland Archives, 1923

Webster, P., *Pétain's Crime*, Macmillan, 1990

West, N. (ed.), *The Guy Liddell Diaries*, Routledge, 2005

Wicklow Commemorating 1798–1998, Wicklow County Council, 1998

Wilder, T., *Bridge of the San Luis Rey*, Longmans & Co., 1927

Willis, N., *Scenery and Antiquities of Ireland*, G. Virtue, 1842

Zeldin, T., *The French*, Collins, 1983

NEWSPAPERS AND PERIODICALS

Belfast Magazine and Literary Journal, 1825

Cork Examiner

Daily Telegraph

Dublin Evening Mail

Evening Herald

Irish Independent

Irish Press

L'Aube

La Dèpèche de Paris

Le Figaro

Le Monde

North Wicklow Newsround

Paris-Presse

Populaire

The Irish Times

The Times

Wicklow People

Wicklow Times